Building Design Systems

Unify User Experiences through a Shared Design Language

Sarrah Vesselov
Taurie Davis

Apress®

Building Design Systems: Unify User Experiences through a Shared Design Language

Sarrah Vesselov
Dade City, FL, USA

Taurie Davis
Portland, OR, USA

ISBN-13 (pbk): 978-1-4842-4513-2
https://doi.org/10.1007/978-1-4842-4514-9

ISBN-13 (electronic): 978-1-4842-4514-9

Managing Director, Apress Media LLC: Welmoed Spahr
Acquisitions Editor: Louise Corrigan
Development Editor: James Markham
Coordinating Editor: Nancy Chen

Cover designed by Taurie Davis

Distributed to the book trade worldwide by Springer Science+Business Media New York, 233 Spring Street, 6th Floor, New York, NY 10013. Phone 1-800-SPRINGER, fax (201) 348-4505, e-mail orders-ny@springer-sbm.com, or visit www.springeronline.com. Apress Media, LLC is a California LLC and the sole member (owner) is Springer Science+Business Media Finance Inc (SSBM Finance Inc). SSBM Finance Inc is a Delaware corporation.

For information on translations, please e-mail rights@apress.com, or visit www.apress.com/rights-permissions.

Apress titles may be purchased in bulk for academic, corporate, or promotional use. eBook versions and licenses are also available for most titles. For more information, reference our Print and eBook Bulk Sales web page at www.apress.com/bulk-sales.

Any source code or other supplementary material referenced by the authors in this book is available to readers on GitHub via the book's product page, located at www.apress.com/9781484245132. For more detailed information, please visit www.apress.com/source-code.

Printed on acid-free paper

Table of Contents

About the Authors

Sarrah Vesselov is a designer and developer with more than 10 years' experience in web design and development. As the UX manager at GitLab, she helped set the overall direction of UX from a design and application experience perspective. Before landing at GitLab, she was lead UX designer and UI developer at Nitro Solutions and UI/UX manager at Mad Mobile, building beautiful experiences for clients including Aeropostale, Payless, Sysco, Talbots, and AutoNation. She served as Director of the Tampa chapter of Women Who Code for several years and is passionate about teaching and mentoring the next generation of tech.

Taurie Davis is a UX and product designer who specializes in applying user-centered design methods to create cohesive, intuitive, and compelling experiences. In her role as Staff UX designer at GitLab, she actively contributed to their design system as a primary maintainer. Her experience includes working with startups and mentoring designers around the world. She is passionate about the open source community and growing open design practices.

About the Technical Reviewer

 **Bermon Painter** has spent the past 20 years focusing on product strategy, design, and web development across a handful of industries. In his current role at EY Digital, Bermon leads innovation initiatives that help organizations create holistic experiences, digital products, and services, with an eye toward delivering value to customers. Bermon is also responsible for building and staffing the EY wavespace™ in Charlotte, a physical innovation space equipped with accelerator programs, co-creation activities, and facilitated design thinking sessions that help teams get in the mindset of approaching challenging problems differently, reinforcing the value of diverse thinking, and creating solutions through rapid prototyping.

As the innovation and strategy lead at EY digital, Bermon applies his expertise in experience strategy, design thinking, agile and lean methodologies, and interface design and development. He frequently speaks at conferences and facilitates workshops around the world. In his local community, Bermon organizes and hosts numerous free community events, hosts a quarterly mini-conference called FusionConf, and leads the Charlotte IxDA chapter.

Before joining EY, Bermon led various cross-discipline teams that crafted holistic product strategies all the way to end-to-end implementation of digital products and services. His claim to fame is having designed the Sass logo. In his free time, he enjoys drinking a tasty frosted mug of root beer while maniacally twisting his mustache.

Acknowledgments

Sarrah and Taurie would like to thank the designers we worked alongside and from whom we learned so much about building design systems: Pedro Moreira da Silva, Dimitrie Hoekstra, Chris Peressini, Matej Latin, Hazel Yang, Jeethu Karthik, and Annabel Dunstone (who pulled double duty between design and front-end).

Thank you to Simon Knox, Winnie Hellmann, and Clement Ho. Your excitement kept our momentum going, and the engineering support was invaluable.

Thank you to Bermon Painter. Your insight made this book that much stronger.

We would like to acknowledge the many industry professionals out there writing and speaking about their work on design systems. When we were first starting our own design systems, your perspective was indispensable and inspired us to share our personal stories and insights here in this book.

Sarrah: Special thanks to my husband, Daniel Urdzik. Without you there to feed me and make me take breaks, I may have died while writing this book. Thank you to my sons, Ni and Maxim Vesselov, for vacating the premises until this book was complete. You can come back now.

Taurie: Special thanks to Lucas Charles for being my constant sounding board, reading and editing chapters countless times, making me endless meals, and giving your full support throughout this entire process. Thank you to Marla Davis for always listening. And last, thanks to Sarrah for sharing this journey with me.

Introduction

When you first begin building a product, the work is fast-paced and exciting. Most of your time is spent heads down, meeting deadlines. The problems you are solving become more evident as you gain a better understanding of the user base. As your comprehension grows, ideas and solutions are formed. Each member of the team has a part to play in crafting the user experience of that product.

The Designer: You have a system for housing design files, but they aren't easily accessible to product managers and developers. Collaborating with those outside of the design department is time-consuming. Screenshots and exported artboards are shared back and forth, and there are constant updates and tweaks required. With no overarching guidelines for your work, you find yourself defending the same choices and solutions over and over again. Looking for the right design file becomes a sport, and it can be hard to remember who worked on what. To make matters worse, you don't feel like you have any real input into the product road map. By the time you become involved, the product manager is focused on a solution rather than the problem being solved.

The Front-end Engineer: Much of your time is spent on developing the same code solutions within different contexts. You try to provide feedback to the design team, but it often feels as though you not only work in different departments, you work on different planets. You don't have access to design files and don't have much insight into the why or how behind the decisions the design team is making. You are noticing inconsistencies in the text, color, and spacing across screens, and the code is a mess.

The Product Manager: There is a lot of pressure from users and other stakeholders to deliver. The road map is long, and the resources are small. It feels as though there aren't enough designers and developers available to handle all the work that needs to be done. There are lots of minor problems you think you can solve on your own, but you don't want to step on anyone's toes. It would be great if the design department could give more input on the road map and vision for the product, but you know they are stretched thin.

Somehow, amid all of this chaos, you need to provide users with a top-notch user experience.

If this sounds familiar, don't worry; you are not alone. As products, teams, and organizations scale, it becomes more difficult to maintain speed and efficiency without a concerted effort. In this book, we will show you how, and when, a design system can be used to solve the problems faced by teams building one product or many.

Design systems offer a way for organizations to build products at scale. Don't let the name fool you; design systems are not just for designers. They benefit the entire organization and offer a foundation for collaboration and innovation. Design systems are a collection of shared principles and practices that help to inform the work of designers, product managers, and engineers, as well as sales and marketing. They offer a single source of truth and are the guiding light for the design and development of a product's user experience.

Why design systems and why now? Design systems are not new. They are the descendant of the traditional graphic standards manual. These printed manuals were a practical way to relay design guidelines for corporation and organizations before the advent of the Internet. Often hefty, these manuals provided the governing principles and practical guidelines for applying a visual language across all areas of a company.

Design systems are the natural evolution of the graphic standards manual for today's organizations. They are the result of the need to coordinate and align the different disciplines necessary to bring digital products to life. These systems do more than merely convey design guidelines such as typeface, logo, or color standards. They unite designers, developers, and product managers along a set of core principles while enabling their work through reusable components.

Throughout our careers, we have been involved in developing many different systems for design. We have watched the evolution from a simple collection of patterns and styles to today's robust systems containing principles, design, and code. Within this book, we've combined our mistakes and successes, in order to share what we have learned every step of the way.

What We'll Cover

We begin by looking at the history of systems in design to gain perspective on how this has affected the design systems of today. You'll learn about the intersection of art, technology, and industry during the early days of the Web and examine the technological advancements that led to the prevalence of CSS and JavaScript in the digital landscape. You'll come to understand why design systems have risen in popularity and how they align with and are influenced by, development best practices.

Next, we will focus on the six interlocking areas that make up a design system; layout, styles, components, regions, content, and usability. You'll learn how these parts work together to create a robust system. We will help you to understand whether it is the right time to implement a design system and, if it is, how to avoid common failures.

Getting support from key stakeholders will be essential. You'll learn about the three target audiences for your system and how to gain their support. You will have to understand how your peers, your overall organization, and the users of your product benefit from a design system, in order to form the necessary allies for your effort. We will also show you how to use qualitative and quantitative data to measure the benefits.

Next, you will learn how to think about design systems as a shared language. You will learn how to create the building blocks and guidelines for your language. This can be done by breaking interfaces down into their simplest forms, as well as by building elements to create larger interfaces. We will show you how to create design principles that you can use to craft your unique design language. These principles will address both user needs and organizational goals.

Implementing your design system can be one of the most difficult hurdles to overcome. We will show you how to assess your organization before attempting to build your system. You'll learn why the type of organization you work for can affect your approach. You'll be given the tools to assess the current state of your product, to help determine the structure that best suits your organization's needs. Case studies help put the unique challenges you are facing into sharper focus.

Iterating on your system will be critical to its future success. Your design system cannot be created and then set aside. You will have to understand how to maintain and scale it as your product and organization changes. Measuring and tracking results will be vital for your stakeholders. We will show you how to maintain momentum through established process, goal setting, and evangelizing your system across your organization.

Finally, we provide you with a detailed case study on the development of GitLab's design system. This case study digs deeply into our roles in building the system, the challenges we faced, and the successes we experienced. An additional chapter audits some of the most popular design systems out there today, giving you insight into the many different methods for structuring your system. Having real-world experiences and resources to draw from will make building your system more straightforward.

Starting your own design system is exciting and daunting. We hope that this book will help make the challenges of building a design system a little less intimidating and a lot more exciting. Let's get started!

CHAPTER 1

The Rise of Design Systems

With the rise of design-led organizations, the role of the designer has shifted from that of mere stylist to that of a business's number-one problem solver. Yet, to build products that people love, designers must do more than solely solve problems. They must structure the way they work, establishing the guiding rules and principles that support and drive both their design process and the product for which they are designing.

If you're reading this book, chances are you don't have to be convinced of the value a design system can bring to your organization. You already know it can make your life and work easier. You believe that consistent design will improve the user experience. You are sure that having established guidelines and usability patterns will enhance communication between team members and simplify the interface for end users.

What you may not be sure of is how to start implementing your design system with the full support of colleagues and upper management. We wrote this book to provide you with the tools necessary to successfully communicate the value a design system can bring to your organization. You will also learn how to establish your own design language, define usability patterns, and create a comprehensive component library.

© Sarrah Vesselov and Taurie Davis 2019
S. Vesselov and T. Davis, *Building Design Systems*,
https://doi.org/10.1007/978-1-4842-4514-9_1

Articles, books, and talks discussing the importance of design systems are rising in popularity (yes, we sense the irony). It may be tempting to write them off as just another design fad that will burn out when the next big thing comes along. However, design systems are not new. Humans have been organizing and categorizing the world around them since the beginning of time. Organization gives us a sense of control and order. Order creates feelings of security and predictability. For some, this predictability feels limiting, something counterintuitive to the vision of creativity and expression. When applied to the world of technology and application design, however, this predictability is freeing, as it removes the need to continuously reinvent the same solutions. By automating and documenting routine tasks, designers have more time for thinking and exploration.

All design systems start the same: as an attempt at making order out of chaos. Categorizing and organizing elements makes them easy to find and replicate. It is a necessary utility, born from the tech industry's need to move fast and innovate even faster. However, design systems are so much more than this. They define the language we use to create new elements and experiences.

A History of Systems in Design

Looking back to the Bauhaus and Swiss design movements, you can begin to see what could be viewed as the foundation for today's design systems. The Bauhaus movement (1919–33) revolved around the idea that "form follows function." Rather than focusing on decorative elements, the primary facet was functional simplicity. The notion that all the parts on a page must have a function led to a focus on proportions, grids, and color theory. An example demonstrating principles from the Bauhaus design movement is shown in Figure 1-1.

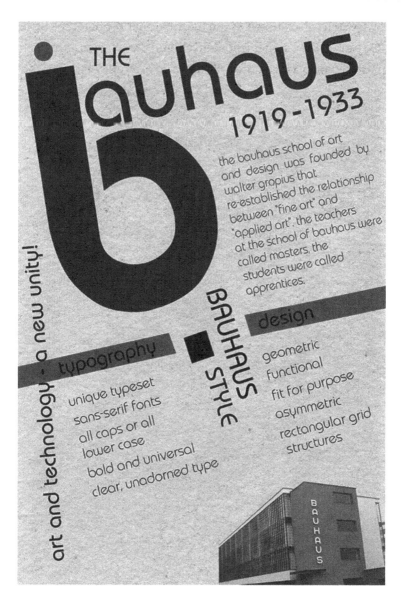

Figure 1-1. *Bauhaus-inspired design by Amna Zulfqar*

The Swiss Style, also known as the International Typographic Style, (1950s–60s) took grids a step further and shifted the focus to asymmetry and clean sans-serif typefaces.[1] Figure 1-2 shows an example of the Swiss Style.

Figure 1-2. *Swiss Style–inspired design by Amna Zulfqar*

---

[1]Rune Madsen, "A History of Design Systems," http://printingcode. runemadsen.com/lecture-intro/.

You may be thinking, How does this relate to design systems? What am I missing? These two crucial periods in art history centered on the idea of a unified design language, with guidelines for patterns and elements that should be followed. They were a fundamental influence on the evolution of modern graphic design, desktop publishing, and, eventually, web design.

The Intersection of Art, Technology, and Industry

Design systems are more than the latest fad; they are a natural evolution in the intersection between art, technology, and industry. Critical factors in this evolution have been:

- The rise of personal computers and the Web.
- Technological advancements in Web development (CSS, JavaScript).
- The influence of technology on business.
- The shift from waterfall to Agile methodologies.

The Rise of the Web

The early days of the Internet were dark for design. Websites were little more than glorified Word documents. In these earlier times, the Web was built using only HTML. CSS did not yet exist, and it was left up to individual browsers to determine how a webpage would be displayed. An early webpage design lacking CSS styling is shown in Figure 1-3.

Figure 1-3. *The Yahoo! home page from 1996 shows an example of an early website lacking CSS styling*

This all began to change in the mid-1990s, as more and more people had access to personal computers and the Internet. Ultimately, this meant that the Web grew in popularity as the place for electronic publishing. Web authors grew increasingly frustrated by the stylistic limitations of HTML. Browsers, recognizing the opportunity this presented, began exploring ways to give authors more control over their pages.

The first proposal for CSS was presented in 1994 and spurred a lot of discussion. Surprisingly, much of the conversation revolved around who should control how a page would be viewed. On the one side, many felt that authors should determine the final presentation, ensuring that it matched their intention and vision. On the other side, some believed that users should have the ability to decide how they would like to view a page (think in terms of things such as preferred font size). These debates spurred the creation of the World Wide Web Consortium (W3C), to help work out standards and best practices for the Web, and, ultimately, HTML and CSS. This was an essential development in the trajectory of the Internet. Without the W3C to unify and make recommendations, each browser could potentially support a different HTML specification.

Technological Advancements

Fast forward a couple of years, and lots of debate, to 1996, when CSS was officially introduced. Microsoft's Internet Explorer was the first browser to support the new technology, with Netscape following close behind.[2] The competition was both good and bad. Good, because browsers were now competing with one another to support Web standards. Bad, because it caused significant pain points for anyone building for the Web. Even as browsers began to support standards, that support was not the same. Each browser implemented CSS in its unique way, causing many inconsistencies. The only thing you could count on was the fact that your webpage would not look the same from browser to browser.

Table-Based Design

As the Web grew, so did the need for better user experience. Graphic designers began to play with this new medium, applying the fundamentals of layout and grid techniques used in print. Even with the adoption and spread of CSS, designing on the Web in these early days was painful and limited. Web layouts were being developed using tables, and there was a lack of control when customizing layouts using HTML and CSS. If you are unfamiliar with tables in HTML, it is the same concept as creating a table inside a Word document. Now, imagine trying to implement a complicated design interface using only images inserted inside table data cells. Some obvious problems arise. Table cells in the same row cannot be different heights, and table cells in the same column cannot be different widths. Web designers had to get very creative, using complicated workarounds of sliced Photoshop images, tables inside of tables, and hidden text, among a variety of other hacks.

---

[2]Bert Bos, "A Brief History of CSS Until 2016," https://www.w3.org/Style/CSS20/history.html, December 17, 2016.

In reaction to table-based layouts, Flash emerged as the gateway program for many graphic designers on the Web. The difficulties posed by the limitations of table-based design presented an opportunity for programs such as Flash to make web applications easier to design. The Flash interface allowed designers to use graphical user interface (GUI) tools to develop rich interactive experiences. It had a profound influence on the Web, raising the bar for design and prompting the development of HTML5, which, in the end, led to Flash's eventual demise.

The Rise of CSS and JavaScript

By 2002, the notion of "table-less design" was beginning to gain momentum. Rather than relying on tables for positioning the elements of a page, CSS had advanced enough to do the job more efficiently. This opened designers up to experimenting with a variety of creative and increasingly complex layouts.

Up until this time, many websites were built page by page. Elements such as the header, footer, and menu were copied and pasted across every page. Change something on one page, and you would have to go to every other page to make the same change. As the complexity and scale of websites increased, performance, scalability, and maintainability became real concerns.

We haven't talked much about JavaScript up to this point. While it has been around for 19 years, its acceptance as one of the pillars of Web development was slow in coming. It gained momentum in the mid-2000s and began to be more heavily relied on for both client-side and server-side development. JavaScript was used to enhance interactivity, performance, and make sites DRY(er).[3] These enhancements opened the floodgates for more complicated and interactive design on the Web.

---

[3]DRY stands for "Don't Repeat Yourself" and is a term used in software engineering. The aim is to reduce repetition and avoid redundancy.

JavaScript also helped to change the way we approach building websites. JavaScript allowed developers to build components rather than entire pages, as demonstrated in Figure 1-4. Components are like Lego bricks that can be moved around to reimagine almost any interface. Reimagining pages and even whole sites became faster and easier. The pace of development picked up quickly, allowing companies to innovate and deliver faster than ever before.

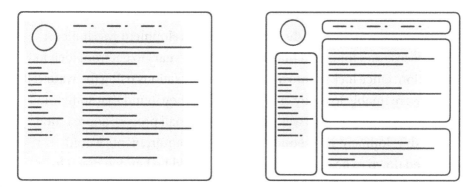

Figure 1-4. *Page-based design vs. component-based design*

This component-based approach is now being adopted by designers on the Web. Design deliverables have changed from whole-page layouts to pieces of the whole. Doing this has its risks. It is easy to get caught up in the details and fail to see the bigger picture. This is where a design system can make all the difference. Defining paradigms makes it easier to keep things consistent and manageable. Well-defined paradigms make everything faster, from design to implementation.

The Influence of Technology on Business

The Internet grew fast, and the number of people buying computers for personal use rose. According to a report from the U.S. Department of Labor, computer ownership in the United States rose from 15% to 35%

between 1990 and 1997.[4] Computers were no longer a luxury; they were a necessity. Organizations immediately recognized the potential of this new information technology market. Many companies were founded during what is known as the dot-com boom. This increase in demand for technology caused a flurry of excitement and a sense of urgency to build bigger, better websites and software products as quickly as possible.

The Move to Agile

The traditional waterfall method of software development was built on heavy process and long lead times. It could take years to get from idea to distribution. Once locked into a concept, organizations using the waterfall process were unable to easily change course if they found that something simply wouldn't work. This was because a waterfall process approached product development in a sequential fashion. Requirements would be handed down to designers, and designs would be handed down to developers, leaving little room for collaboration among teams. Without this collaboration in place, it was extremely difficult to shift directions when problems arose later in the process.

In 2001, frustrated with the lack of progress, thought leaders gathered to find a more efficient way to develop technology products.[5] This was the birth of Agile, a fast-delivery approach to building software. It allowed organizations to deliver their products quickly, with full knowledge that they may not have gotten it right the first time. They could then gather user feedback and make improvements in rapid succession. Agile focuses on the people building and using the software and not the process or tools it takes to make that software.

---

[4]U.S. Department of Labor, Bureau of Labor Statistics, "Issues in Labor Statistics," `https://www.bls.gov/opub/btn/archive/computer-ownership-up-sharply-in-the-1990s.pdf`, March 1999.

[5]Kent Beck et al., "Manifesto for Agile Software Development," `https://agilemanifesto.org/`, 2001.

Tying It All Together

The rise of component-based architectures and the move to Agile software development has created a need for design systems. With so much of our design work focused on small pieces of the product, it is easy to lose sight of the whole. Design systems provide a necessary overview of the product, its goals, and driving vision. It details the language used to build and design, enabling your team to work faster and more confidently. Additionally, design systems provide an iterative snapshot of your interface and are an essential wayfinding tool for engineering, product, and design.

In the next chapter, we will take a closer look at what makes up a design system and how to decide if and when your organization truly needs one. We will also discuss why and how design systems can fail and what you can do to protect your team from failure.

CHAPTER 2

Introducing Design Systems

Understanding the goal of a design system is the first step toward implementing a solution that helps teams successfully scale product. With a clearly defined system, designers and engineers can focus their efforts on solving user needs, rather than re-creating elements and reinventing solutions.

Throughout this book, we'll discuss six interlocking areas that make up a design system.

- **Layout**: Defined measures that make up your spacing and grid system.

- **Styles**: Core aspects of your visual language. These include colors, iconography, and typography.

- **Components**: Core elements of an interface. These include buttons and form fields.

- **Regions**: Overarching design paradigms, such as navigation or search.

- **Content**: Information regarding the voice and tone, as well as punctuation guidelines. Content can also include terminology if your product has a specific vocabulary.

- **Usability**: Rules that define accessibility and internationalization.

© Sarrah Vesselov and Taurie Davis 2019
S. Vesselov and T. Davis, *Building Design Systems*,
https://doi.org/10.1007/978-1-4842-4514-9_2

These parts work together, building off one another. For example, components are created with a combination of both layout and style, while regions are composed of multiple components, as shown in Figures 2-1 through 2-3. Content informs the copy used within your components, while usability keeps the content accessible. The size and scope of these areas can vary, depending on the organization, but all should be considered.

Throughout this book, we will use the following terms when referencing different aspects within your system:

- **Elements**: The lowest-level object. Elements cannot be broken down further. This can include labels and icons.

- **Components**: A combination of one or more elements that function as a whole, such as a form.

- **Component groups**: A group of components that form a larger component, as seen in Figure 2-2.

Figure 2-1. *Spacing (layout), combined with color and typography (styles), create components*

Figure 2-2. *Components can be combined to form component groups. In this example, combined buttons create a segmented control. Another example includes combining an input field with a button to create a form.*

Figure 2-3. *Multiple components can create larger paradigms used throughout your product, such as navigation. It is helpful to document guidelines related to these specific regions.*

Style Guides, Component Libraries, and Design Systems

As design tools become more sophisticated, style guides and component libraries continue to grow in popularity. This popularity is for a good reason, as they allow designers to create core elements that can be shared and synced across multiple design files. By making a change in one file, you can easily update the design across all files that use that same element. This allows designers to easily make global changes and achieve consistency within their design tool.

A common misconception is that style guides, component libraries, and design systems are all the same. This confusion occurs because often, they contain many of the same parts. A primary difference is that a design system houses the processes and philosophies behind your design decisions. Your design system is a documented approach to systematic design. Style guides and component libraries are assets to help get you there. In addition, the core of a design system is tied to the codebase of your application, whereas style guides and component libraries are often static. With design systems, components are built, implemented, and documented with the help of front-end engineers. This is an important distinction that ultimately helps your team develop a series of components that can easily be referenced, used, and updated directly within your codebase. Design systems let teams move faster by reducing the layers of translation between design and implementation.

- **Style guide**: Static documentation that defines how the brand is stylistically applied to interface elements. It contains high-level details about color, typography, iconography, and more.

- **Component library**: A set of styles and components that can be used and shared among a team. A component library consists of common core elements that are used throughout an application. If supported by a design tool, they can automatically sync across design files when a change is made. Component libraries may or may not include living code.

- **Design system**: A series of documented elements, components, and regions that include both design and front-end guidelines. The documentation contains live code examples, allowing cross-functional teams to easily reuse styles and components in several instances across an application. A design system also includes underlying design principles, rules, and guidelines that help a team build one or multiple products.

Our experience   The terms *components* and *patterns* are often used interchangeably. For example, a component library is often also called a pattern library.

Terminology is important, but don't get too caught up on exact phrases. Define terms based on what works for your organization and be consistent in how you use them within your team.

The Right Time to Implement a Design System

There are a few factors to take into consideration when deciding if it is the right time to implement a design system. You'll want to consider the following:

- Age of the organization.

- Team size.

- Volume and type of work.

Age of the Organization

In the beginning, many organizations invest more time and effort into growing products and features than they do in developing good user interfaces. It is easy to point fingers, but the climate for technology and the speed at which companies must move to become profitable can make even the smartest organization choose features over experience.

Putting a design system in place takes a great deal of time and effort. According to a 2018 design systems survey conducted by Figma, design systems typically come after the product is built.[1] Creating patterns and strict guidelines are often unnecessary during the early stages of a startup or in a young organization. Attempting to lock the team into a set of strict guidelines while everything is still in flux will result in wasted time, as the organization pivots to meet market demands.

That isn't to say you can't begin to lay the foundations for a design system. This is the time to loosely organize patterns and guidelines. Establish a single source of truth for the basics, such as typography, colors, and spacing, but avoid creating too much overhead and process. Until things are more stable, it will be important to remain flexible.

---

[1]Figma, "State of Design Systems 2018," https://www.figma.com/blog/state-of-design-systems-2018/, December 19, 2018.

17

Team Size

If there are only a few designers and engineers on your team, it may be too early to start thinking about a design system. Keep in mind the resources that you have. A small team might mean you are strapped for time. Being unable to spend sufficient time to start your system could result in failure. If you anticipate that the team will be growing soon, now is the time to think about how you will handle that growth. Keeping things organized and preparing only the essential documentation should suffice. Once the team grows to five or more members, it is likely time to think about a more sophisticated system.

It is equally important to think about other teams you interact with. Will a design system improve communication and collaboration with product, development, and even marketing? If the answer is yes, then it is time!

Volume and Type of Work

At first glance, agency work may seem too varied and fast-paced to benefit from a design system. The work is continually changing and can vary significantly from day to day. Designers must often context switch between different sets of branding guidelines and user bases. Compared to that of a product team, the work does not have a regular cadence of iteration, and designers don't typically have the opportunity to grow the user experience steadily over time. However, a design system can be used as a starting point for creating brand-consistent user experiences at agency speed. Many agencies can use a generic set of layout rules, components, and regions that can be easily adapted to each brand's unique look and feel. In some cases, agencies will even build unique design systems for their clients.

Approaching the Start of Your Design System

In the beginning, implementing a design system can feel overwhelming. Understanding the current state of your product is always a good first step toward incrementally building your design system.

Whether your organization is young or mature, starting with an interface inventory will provide insight into where you are in the process of creating your system. The goal of your inventory is to assess the layout, styles, and components used throughout your product. It can also serve as a road map when defining the scope of your design system.

A component library can be used as a first step toward incrementally implementing your design system. You and your design team can work from the interface inventory to create a series of components that are then used to communicate with your front-end engineering team during implementation.

A design system is distinct for every organization. To begin planning, ask yourself fundamental questions to understand the needs and goals of your organization and users. Some of these questions may include:

- What details prevent our team from quickly and efficiently creating designs?

- How does our visual language complement brand guidelines?

- Which components are most frequently used?

- Which interactions are critical to core business needs?

- Does our organization support internationalization?

- Who is our user base and how can we enable them to use the product effectively?

- What tone do we use to communicate with users?

Questions such as these map long-term goals to the six interlocking areas that make up a design system. Asking the right questions also helps break down the needs of your organization into small, digestible pieces, making it easier to get started and stay motivated.

Note   To learn more about implementation techniques, see Chapter 5.

Understanding Why Design Systems Fail

Design systems are not foolproof. They can fail for many reasons. Understanding how and why things can go wrong will help you stay on track.

Lack of Initial Buy-In

Attempting to build anything without the support of your organization will be a struggle. Building a design system requires resources and time. You can't do it all on your own. Before making any decisions or taking any steps, take the time to talk to others in your organization. Start by getting a feel for what they already may know about design systems. Approach conversations from the perspective of problem-solving: What pain points do they encounter that a design system would help relieve? What goals and initiatives are important to them, and how can a design system further those goals?

Make sure to reach out to colleagues at every level of the organization: product management, engineering, sales, marketing, and executive leadership. It is essential that everyone understands the specific benefits a design system will provide them. You must evangelize and then socialize your design system; otherwise, you run the risk of others seeing it as a design-only initiative and losing support for the time and resources needed.

> **Note**   To learn more about getting support for your design system, see Chapter 3.

Trying to Do Too Much, Too Soon

Getting started on your design system is exciting, but don't let that excitement get the better of you and your team. It can be tempting to jump right into working on your system. It is vital to understand your company's unique needs and challenges before devoting all your time and resources to building something.

Pace yourself and your team, or you run the risk of burning out. Understand what you really need before committing, and accept the fact that progress may not always be as fast as you would like. Doing a lot and then nothing can make both stakeholders and your team lose faith in your system.

> **Note**   To learn more about framing your design system, see Chapter 3.

Perfectionism

Don't try to make your system perfect by worrying over every little detail. Iteration will be vital to getting your design system up and running. As you work, you will discover patterns you forgot or details that seem vital. Keep a running list of improvements and additions. Avoid the impulse to switch gears to get them in your system immediately. Approach building your design system as you would any other project. Plan, execute, and iterate as new information or needs arise. Most of all, get comfortable with the idea that it will never be "done."

> **Note**   To learn how to implement your system iteratively, see Chapter 5.

Maintenance

It is common to feel the pressure to deliver quickly, both for your team and external stakeholders. Don't give in to this pressure. Think strategically when developing your design system. Avoid getting stuck with a system that requires constant upkeep. Such things as static images and repeated text will not scale as your system grows and becomes more complicated. Self-documentation is essential if you want to ensure the system remains relevant.

> **Note**   To learn more about building a maintainable design system, see Chapters 5 and 6.

Design System Envy

Getting inspiration from other design systems can be extremely helpful. You can see how other companies have grouped their content, which components are vital to include, as well as how much and what information is necessary to document. However, it is hard not to compare your progress to more prominent organizations, and that can be demotivating. You may have only a few people in your organization available to work on your system part-time. Remember that many of the well-established design systems you see have been developed over a period of years by full-time, devoted teams. Be happy with your progress and concentrate on the needs of your organization.

Note   To learn how to use other design systems to your advantage, see Chapter 8.

Tying It All Together

Six interlocking areas make up a design system: layout, styles, components, regions, content, and usability. A robust design system should contain guiding design principles, guidelines for use and implementation, as well as a component library that includes front-end code.

Before you build anything, determine whether it is the right time to implement a design system. Avoid investing a lot of time creating a design system before your team and organization are ready for it. You may have to start gradually, beginning with a style guide and basic UI kit. As your team and organization grow, so will the need for a design system.

When you are ready, start with an interface inventory of your product. Document the layouts, styles, and components that make up your unique interface. Then, ask some fundamental questions to understand the needs and goals of your organization and its user base. Answers to these questions will allow you to map out the long-term goals of your system.

Finally, knowing why design systems fail is as essential as knowing what makes them successful. Avoid the common traps, such as perfectionism, taking on too much, and starting a system without proper buy-in from stakeholders.

CHAPTER 3

Selling the System

Often, it can be difficult to articulate to others something that you know intuitively. As designers, it is our job not only to create better user experiences but also to explain why they are better, in the simplest terms possible. More often than not, we are not the decision makers within an organization. To see our ideas come to pass, we have to advocate for them to the decision makers. We can't just be convinced of the value of our ideas; we have to show that value to others.

Design systems feel intuitive to designers. Perhaps this is a byproduct of being problem solvers. We naturally seek out problems and ways to solve them. Design systems feel like a natural solution to the many obstacles that come from working on projects at scale.

Whether formally or not, we have all designed systems with the intent of making our jobs or lives more comfortable and enjoyable. Tapping into this idea is the first step in communicating the value a design system can bring to an organization.

Defining Why Design Systems Are Beneficial

Every organization is unique, both in its offerings and its challenges. Communicating the value and benefit a design system can bring in a relatable way is critical. Approach it as you would a product problem. The first step is to understand the organization, its goals, and challenges, as well as individual roles and the parts they play.

© Sarrah Vesselov and Taurie Davis 2019
S. Vesselov and T. Davis, *Building Design Systems*,
https://doi.org/10.1007/978-1-4842-4514-9_3

What are the goals of the organization? How can you align user experience goals with those of the broader organization? Who will benefit most from a well-defined system? These are all essential questions to answer.

Three Dimensions of Value

To begin answering these questions, let's examine the value of a design system in light of who will benefit and how. Generally, you can break it down into three target audiences: the employees of the organization, the users of the product, and the organization itself.

Selling Value at the Employee Level

We will start with the benefits to employees first, because, let's face it, making employees' lives comfortable and enjoyable has benefits for all three target audiences. We surveyed 82 people with questions relating to their skills, personal and professional goals, as well as what frustrates them most in their work. We used this data to build simple personas that will help you to understand how each role benefits from a design system.

Designers

The majority of designers (Table 3-1) we spoke with placed problem solving and elevating the perception of design at the top of their priorities list. Many of them felt frustrated and held back by vague requirements, too many meetings, and the pressure to deliver solutions quickly without proper discovery. Design systems can help alleviate these frustrations while enabling designers to move faster and be more productive.

Table 3-1. *Designer Persona*

A.K.A.	• UX designer • UX engineer • Interactive designer • Product designer • Multimedia designer
How I see what I do	• I make sure we are solving the right problems. I use data to understand user needs and motivations as a way of delivering the best experience possible.
My core skills	• Design • Research • Communication • Collaboration • Problem solving • T-shaped skills: broad knowledge of design concepts with deep knowledge of certain disciplines (e.g., interactive design, research, visual design)
My personal goals	• Continue to learn and push the quality of my design solutions • Work on design solutions that have a positive impact on people • Keep up with design trends and technologies to remain relevant in the industry
My professional goals	• Help others see the value and effectiveness of good design • Solve user problems • Create solutions that make a difference in people's lives • Bring together user experience and visual appeal

(*continued*)

Table 3-1. (*continued*)

I spend most of my time on	• Meetings
	• Design discussion/discovery
	• Documentation
	• Defending/advocating for my design solutions
	• Communicating with other teams to better understand the problem
Things that frustrate me	• Meetings
	• Out-of-date documentation
	• Lack of understanding or support for the value of design
	• Vague requirements
	• Lack of support/trust from product owners
	• Pressure to deliver quickly without proper research or discovery

An established system gives the design team access to styles, shared components, and implementation guidelines. This single source of truth helps the team to work independently of one another while ensuring consistency. Shared design documents allow designers to quickly and accurately put together high-fidelity designs.

Design systems also give designers the opportunity to step outside of their traditional toolset and create prototypes in the browser. Doing so enables them to see what will be in production instead of the "ideal world" within a design tool. Some design systems make components available in the browser, allowing designers to quickly and easily change attributes and behaviors without knowing how to code. Other systems require the use of Git and running the project locally to create prototypes. Designers can quickly learn how to do this on their own or work in tandem with an engineer. Many designers are getting comfortable with component wrapping and styling, learning how to handle these changes without the aid of engineers. A design system brings designers closer to the final product earlier in the process, allowing them to test solutions and iterate faster.

Design systems can make space for innovation and creativity. How can devoting time and energy to a design system make a design team more innovative and creative? It may seem counterintuitive, but, in the end, a well-thought-out design system buys the team time. Designers will have time to dedicate to exploration and idea generation rather than to solving the same set of user-experience problems over and over again. The design team is now in a position to do more user research, explore user journeys, and investigate ways to make the existing experience more intuitive and competitive. The organization, its user base, and the design team all benefit from this ability to dig more deeply into the product.

It will be important to emphasize this, as there will be a trade-off in the beginning. It could potentially take a significant amount of time to establish the design system. Stressing that this is temporary and that the team stands to gain that time back plus some can help soothe these concerns.

Engineers

The engineers (Table 3-2) we spoke with gave surprisingly similar answers as the designers. Too many meetings, inadequate requirements, and missing design assets were among their chief complaints. As with designers, there was a personal need to engage in fulfilling work that utilized their creativity to solve everyday problems. The benefits design systems bring to engineers are clear. They clarify solutions, make assets readily available, and give engineers the tools to create autonomously.

Table 3-2. *Engineer Persona*

A.K.A.	• Support engineer • Front-end engineer • Web developer • Software engineer • QA • Back-end engineer
How I see what I do	• I listen to problems and solve them. I troubleshoot all the things and automate everything possible. I create, support, and expand upon solutions.
My core skills	• Development • Communication • Collaboration • Problem solving • T-shaped skills: broad knowledge of programming and development with deep knowledge of particular languages or problem spaces (e.g., infrastructure, databases, etc.)
My personal goals	• Keep up with ever-changing tech processes and requirements, to remain relevant in the industry • Encourage mutual interest and respect between collaborating roles • Deliver useful things • Use programming as a creative outlet and get paid for it
My professional goals	• Minimize customizations while meeting user and business needs • Minimize risk and technical debt • Build scalable, maintainable code

(*continued*)

Table 3-2. (*continued*)

I spend most of my time on	• Communicating with product managers, project managers, designers, and clients
	• Clarifying requirements
	• Meetings
	• Setting up dev environments
	• Learning something new for a project I am working on
Things that frustrate me	• Meetings
	• Maintaining documentation
	• Complicated dev environments
	• Lack of transparency across departments/teams
	• Bad requirements and lack of discovery
	• Missing assets

The design-to-developer handoff is an additional source of frustration for many. Designers often have to create detailed specs, such as redlined designs[1], for every design handed off to a developer. Done manually, this is a time-consuming process. With an established system, design specs remain consistent and can be automatically documented and generated. Developers can use these guidelines as a reference during the implementation phase, cutting down on the need for a back and forth with designers. With detailed documentation, developers will be able to copy the code for the component they require and move on.

Product

Product managers (Table 3-3) set the product vision and strategy. This vision occurs on two distinct levels: the macro and the micro. At the macro-level, the focus is on the whole application. This includes flows,

---

[1]Redlined designs are specs that are generated by designers which place red lines on top of mockups to indicate the sizing and spacing of elements.

features, and overall stability. At the micro-level, the focus shifts to small-scale interactions. Maintaining a holistic (macro) view of an application while focusing on the details (micro) can be a challenge for anyone. Design systems help reduce the cognitive load spent on micro-level interactions, allowing product managers to focus on the larger picture.

Table 3-3. *Product Persona*

A.K.A.	• Product owner • Product manager
How I see what I do	• I work with executive leadership, designers, engineers, and our user base to determine the features that will fulfill the vision and needs of the product. I solve everyday problems.
My core skills	• Communication • Collaboration • Research • Problem solving • T-shaped skills: broad knowledge of design, engineering, and business concepts with deep knowledge of their particular industry and user base
My personal goals	• Continually learn about new technologies • Improve my ability to see the bigger picture and direction • Improve my ability to communicate and gain buy-in from key players
My professional goals	• Solve customer problems while propelling the needs and goals of the business • Understand my users better than anyone else • Understand all the players (design, engineering, sales, executives, etc.) better than anyone else • Understand my industry better than anyone else

(continued)

Table 3-3. (*continued*)

I spend most of my time on	• Product discussion/discovery • Reviewing data • Meeting with customers • Communicating with other teams to keep features and improvements coming
Things that frustrate me	• Lack of understanding or support for valuable features • Inability to work directly on features or problems (i.e., contribute code or design)

It isn't uncommon for product managers and developers to outnumber UX designers at an organization. This situation can sometimes cause tension and, potentially, trust issues, as UX becomes a "blocker" for improvements. As an example, imagine that a product manager has an idea for a feature but the UX team has other priorities. Instead of waiting, the product manager pushes ahead with an MVC (minimal viable content) that contradicts existing patterns. The instinct from UX can be to put their foot down and say, "everything must come through us."

Well-documented usability patterns and usage guidelines make it easy for product managers to make educated decisions without the burden of UX oversight. A design system does the heavy lifting by making common usability patterns, usage guidelines, and defined styles available at any time. The ability to cross-reference the details of an interface or interaction with those generally used across the application can save hours of time for UX and product managers.

Sales

The bar for application design is high. Potential users want to know that what they are buying has the features they need and that they won't get frustrated using it. The sales department (Table 3-4) often reaches out to product and engineering teams to get answers to questions that can determine whether a deal will go through. A design system provides greater visibility into the product, giving sales teams insight into the organization's unique direction.

Table 3-4. *Sales Persona*

A.K.A.	• Sales account manager • Sales representative • Solutions architect • Sales admin • Account manager
How I see what I do	• I build relationships with people. I make their lives easier by understanding their needs and communicating that back to the organization.
My core skills	• Communication • Good listening skills • Product knowledge • Prospecting
My personal goals	• Deliver what customers really want and need • Money is not the most important thing, but it is a motivator for me and my work. • To be liked, respected, and recognized by my peers
My professional goals	• Solve customer problems while propelling the needs and goals of the business • Dedicate myself to ensuring my client's success • Make and exceed my sales quotas on a regular basis • Achieve revenue targets

(*continued*)

Table 3-4. (*continued*)

I spend most of my time on	• Client calls and meetings • Logistics for meetings • Demos • Communicating with marketing and product about ways to increase sales and make the product more valuable to the customer
Things that frustrate me	• Waiting to get answers to customer questions from product or engineering • Lack of urgency internally and externally • Not having enough time to research and learn

Marketing

As in the case of sales, the marketing department (Table 3-5) is focused on how to best frame the product, its offerings, and its competitive advantages. Through a design system, marketing can become more aligned with its product counterparts. This ultimately helps shape a cohesive design language used throughout the organization.

Table 3-5. *Marketing Persona*

A.K.A	• Content marketing associate • Marketing director • Marketing executive • Social media strategist • Brand manager
How I see what I do	• I work for the organization and the customer. I create a sense of excitement and shape brands through engaging content and targeted campaigns.

(*continued*)

Table 3-5. (*continued*)

My core skills	• Communication • Good listening skills • Good writing skills • Product knowledge • Market and industry knowledge
My personal goals	• Maintain a sense of creativity and inspiration in my work • Keep up with the constantly changing landscape of Internet marketing
My professional goals	• Increase market share • Attract and retain customers • Achieve marketing goals • Build a consistent and compelling brand experience
I spend most of my time on	• Logistics for campaigns, events, and projects • Market and industry research • Measuring results • Communicating results with the executive team • Understanding the product vision to better represent the brand
Things that frustrate me	• Lack of urgency internally and externally • When an organization does not follow through on its commitments • Constantly changing targets • Inability to accurately measure results • Impossible deadlines • Not having enough time to research and learn

In our survey, the sales and marketing groups shared similar goals and frustrations. Both voiced frustration with the lack of opportunity to learn more about the product itself. A design system can be used for onboarding, as it defines common terminology, concepts, and patterns unique to the product. Sales and marketing can utilize the system to learn about and familiarize themselves with the product and organizational language.

Both groups also pointed to a lack of urgency from others as a blocker. It isn't uncommon for sales prospects to question the future of specific features or request enhancements before committing to the purchase. A design system can be used to quickly answer these concerns and demonstrate to potential buyers the future vision and direction for the product. It showcases the organization's commitment to continually improving the user experience.

Shared Vision and Language

A good starting point is to emphasize design systems as a language. Each language is unique to the organization and the product. Documenting this language and establishing a clear vision decreases the likelihood of miscommunication and makes it easier for employees across the organization to contribute to better user experiences. The design, product, development, sales, and marketing teams all stand to benefit.

Making this language accessible to all employees increases consistency and empowers all teams to be part of improving the user experience. There is no need for other teams to overstep boundaries or inadvertently work against UX if the design language is available to all.

Note   To learn more about crafting your language, see Chapter 4.

Quick Onboarding for All New Team Members

Whether you are starting on the UX team, joining the engineering department, or beginning in marketing, a design system can be an excellent jumping-off point. It maintains an overview of the application design and terminologies used, while also providing an easy way for anyone to understand the organization's unique language. For those starting in design or development, readily available components allow you to jump in on day one and contribute.

Selling Value at the Organizational Level

In the beginning, many organizations invest more time and effort into growing features than they do into developing good user interfaces. As designers, it can be frustrating to have a seat at the table but feel no power while in that seat. Pressure to push out results can make you feel as though you are a consultant rather than a partner—a checkbox in a process rather than a driver.

Many of the most successful companies are design-driven or have a deep appreciation for the value good design can bring. A study published by McKinsey & Company[2] in 2018 found a strong correlation between how capable a company is at design and how well it performs financially. Apple, Airbnb, Slack, and IBM come to mind quickly. These companies have invested time and resources into design, with design leadership existing in the C-suite.

Unfortunately, this is not a common occurrence. For many of us, design and its concerns in the organization linger in the middle management layer. We have to consistently advocate for design by speaking a shared language.

---

[2]Benedict Sheppard et al., "The business value of design," *McKinsey Quarterly*, https://www.mckinsey.com/business-functions/mckinsey-design/our-insights/the-business-value-of-design, October 2018.

Speaking in terms of ROI

How can design teams in organizations without executive design leadership effectively make a case for a design system? Work on describing the benefits of a design system in quantifiable terms when selling the idea at the executive level. Many organizations will say that they value user experience, but when it comes down to it, things like the performance and stability of the product are regarded separately and as a higher priority than user experience. Uptime and availability are readily obtainable measurements. It is easy to quantify the return on investment (ROI) for achieving 100% uptime. It can be more challenging to measure user satisfaction accurately.

Merely saying that a design system will increase consistency or improve user experience is not something most business executives, or even product managers, will see as a tangible benefit. You need to speak their language and describe the benefits in terms of ROI, as follows:

- What does the organization stand to gain from the time and money being spent?

- How will a design system increase revenue, customer retention, and productivity?

Let's look at an example. Imagine that your organization has developed an ambitious road map for next year. The number of features planned would require the whole team full-time, leaving no room for improving the existing feature set. You know that having a design system would help automate a significant portion of the effort. This automation would allow for the exploration and designing of new features as well as improving existing ones.

- Select just one of the features and estimate the number of hours it will take to explore, design, and build from scratch.

- Now, estimate the time it would take if you had the following:

  - Components (design and code, readily available for product, engineering, and UX)

  - Consistent guidelines and standards, including specs (faster reviews for quality and assurance)

- Measure the difference and multiply this number by the total number of features proposed. Some features will be larger, and some will be smaller. Don't worry about that. We are looking for a rough estimate here. Got it? Good!

- Now, multiply the total number of hours by the average designer's hourly rate.

The result is an estimate of how much time a design system will save and how much money that time is worth to the organization.

There are many ways to show the value of your design system. Finding ways to tie this value into revenue and profit will make a more compelling case. Using the worksheet provided later in this chapter, review your organization's goals. If a particular feature or feature set represents the anchor for sales and marketing efforts, improving the user experience of this feature is likely to increase retention and revenue. Mapping UX goals to the organizational goals in this way can make it easier to demonstrate the return for investing time and money into a design system.

Get a Baseline from Employees and Users

It isn't enough to say that something will have an impact. You should have a plan for measuring the results to demonstrate positive effects. Use both quantitative and qualitative methods of measurement when evaluating the effectiveness of your improvements. To do this, you will have to gather baseline data early, so be prepared to factor this into your plan.

- Establish the current level of satisfaction that users have, through surveys and usability testing. Use a System Usability Scale (SUS)[3] template to measure the usability of your product.

- Remember: The goals are to highlight the benefits across all user groups. This includes measuring user satisfaction across multiple areas of the product, as well as employee satisfaction with the current system.

Note   For additional information on gathering baseline data, see Chapter 6.

Maintain and Update Data

Continue to do research throughout the process of implementing the design system. As the system becomes more robust and covers more areas of the product, the overall ROI should improve. The goal is to show that employees are more productive and happier with their work and that users

---

[3]To learn more about SUS visit https://www.usability.gov/how-to-and-tools/methods/system-usability-scale.html

are more productive and more satisfied with the product. If your results do not bear this out, this is your opportunity to reevaluate and take corrective action early on. Remember to:

- Have a plan for continued measurement and evaluation.

- Compare baseline data from your initial testing with subsequent testing.

- Keep track of corrective actions, to ensure they have the desired effect.

Cost and Agility

The need to get to market before the competition has dramatically changed software development. In today's agile environment, we no longer have the luxury of lengthy discovery and exploration. There is great emphasis placed on speed and cost-effectiveness, so much so that we are often working on discovery, design, and implementation all at once.

There are many ways to cut costs within an organization. It isn't uncommon for design departments to be the first to feel the pinch when organizations have to cut back. But what *appears* to provide savings could end up costing the organization a lot more in the long run. Robert Pressman illustrates this point beautifully in his book *Software Engineering: A Practitioner's Approach*: "For every dollar spent to resolve a problem during product design, $10 would be spent on the same problem during development, and multiply to $100 or more if the problem had to be solved after the product's release."[4]

Design systems present an opportunity to reduce costs without resorting to layoffs or slashing benefits. Established patterns and guidelines have already been thought out, tested, and used in other areas

---

[4]Roger S.Pressman, *Software Engineering: A Practitioner's Approach* (New York: McGraw-Hill) 1987.

of the application. Leveraging these patterns will reduce the cycle time from design to implementation and be more likely to provide a superior user experience the first time.

Our experience   Identifying key features or areas of the application that will be improved is one way to quantifiably present value. Pairing work on the design system with organizational goals masks the time involved. You are still putting in the time and effort, but in a way that appears more productive to the rest of the company. Optics are important.

Selling Value at the User Level

Don't forget the primary beneficiary of a well-thought-out design system: the end user. Delighting users is what will often determine the success of a product. The overall usability of a product, coupled with the benefits it offers a user, is critical.

All of the benefits listed in our other sections trickle down to benefit the user:

- Happy and more productive employees have more time to work on complex flows and user experience solutions.

- Reduced cycle time allows improved experiences to make it into the product faster, increasing feedback and further iteration.

- Sales and marketing can appropriately address buyer concerns and questions before users are locked in.

Communication Strategies

Communication is all about balance—a balance between talking and listening, educating and learning. There are many methods and channels you can use to communicate with your team, colleagues, and bosses about your design system. The methods include diplomacy, education, salesmanship, and good public relations (PR). The channels include, but are not limited to, organizational announcements, one-on-one conversations, and updates to guidelines and handbooks. Balancing these methods and channels will give you the greatest likelihood of success.

Diplomacy

Engage with other teams and key players within the company. Most important will be members of product and front-end engineering, as they will be the first to reap the rewards of the system. They may also be your staunchest allies.

Diplomacy is not about politicking or quid pro quos. Diplomacy is about understanding and defining the expectations of both you and your colleagues. Build trust and be flexible. Listen to their needs and make a concerted effort to find the balance between your needs and theirs. Not only will it help ensure support from other departments, it will also help to better inform and shape your design system.

As a part of diplomacy, you'll have to educate those around you about what it is you are proposing. Don't assume what others know, or don't know, about design systems. Practice empathic listening when speaking about your design system. Don't expect that they have understood what you have said. Try to put yourself in their place and listen from their point of view. Look at their body language and pay attention to the questions they ask. No matter how well you think you are messaging your intentions, they may not be understood.

Use multiple channels to get your message across and get feedback on what others understand from these communications. Use one-on-ones, team meetings, and organizational announcements to advocate how your design system will benefit the organization and its employees.

Education

There are many misconceptions surrounding design systems. Ensuring that you, your team, and the remainder of your organization have a shared understanding of what a design system is will be crucial to its success.

The most common misconception is that style guides and design systems are the same thing. Design systems and style guides do have similar goals, both serve to create a unified and consistent style across an application. However, style guides are just one piece of a whole. They don't represent a design system in and of itself. A fully realized design system is a language shared amongst an organization. It is composed of the design concepts, terminologies, and the overall approach the organization takes in communicating ideas.

This concept can be challenging to get across, especially for those outside of the design department in an organization. It may be helpful to explain that a design system is a set of connected parts and principles. It will contain the voice and vision for design at the organization. This could roughly be compared to an organization's mission statement. It will provide the terminology and definitions for UI elements used throughout the product, as well as make available common usability patterns. Once there is a basic understanding of what a design system is, it is easier to communicate the benefits and value it will bring.

Salesmanship: Preparing for the "No"

Preparing yourself for the objections and reservations of others will help you address their concerns and, hopefully, win them over. Be positive, but realistic, about the reactions you are likely to receive.

The following are a few reasons why stakeholders will say "no":

- **We don't have enough resources to devote to this effort**. Create a survey to show just how much time employees are spending on fixing UI bugs or how much time developers are spending asking designers to review basic UX paradigms. Show them the wasted resources and explain that the design system will begin to shift these resources to more productive areas.

- **We can't stop shipping features to organize. It will never be finished**. Recognize that they are right, and it will never be complete, but that's okay! Improving the user experience should never be finished. You should always be striving for the best product that solves user needs in the most efficient way. Acknowledge the truth of their statement and explain how you can start by building the documentation for areas you are working on now. There is no need to stop the work being done on current features. Simply ensure that, moving forward, all documentation will be done as features are developed.

- **We don't see the value. How does this help our product and UX?** Design systems focus effort on improving the overall product rather than keeping the focus on redesigning the same features over and over again. Driving efforts toward achieving organizational objectives will, in the end, translate to user experience improvements for the end user. It will align teams using a common language and make design, product, engineering, marketing, and sales all more productive and united. People are more readily able to make autonomous decisions, which means the organization moves faster as a whole.

Good Public Relations!

As you may have already experienced, implementing a design system requires positive PR within your organization. The good news is that design systems have the potential to be PR in and of themselves. Airbnb and Google are excellent examples of this. When you establish a unique design language for your product, people begin to see them as lifestyles instead of just a product they use. They get excited about releases and want to hear about what you are working on.

Many organizations go so far as to open-source their design systems, driving further interest in their product as a resource beyond a service. Good public relations is just one more selling point when trying to get internal buy-in for your design system.

Selling Your System Worksheet

Now that you've learned about all the different ways to communicate the value of your design system, it's time to craft the pitch that's right for your organization. We've put together this worksheet to help you understand organizational goals, map those goals to UX design goals, and identify your allies. Think of this business case as a road map to crafting convincing arguments when talking about your design system.

1. What is/are the long-term goal(s) of the organization? Is it an acquisition, going public, etc.?

2. What is the goal of the organization for the coming year? This could be in the form of OKRs (Objective and Key Results), KPIs (Key Performance Indicators), or however your organization tracks and measures success.[5]

3. What are the current efforts the UX team is making to achieve the organizational goals, both short-term and long-term?

4. Now, look at your answers to 1, 2, and 3. Identify how a design system can support these efforts and write them down. If you are unsure, consult a colleague for insight.

5. Are there specific areas of the product needing work that can be coupled with development of the design system? For example, perhaps you have long settings pages that desperately need to be cleaned up with the use of better spacing, form styling, and sectioning. Work on this area and document the updated spacing, form styles, and sections in the system. Push to have these new usability patterns and styling implemented throughout the product.

---

[5]OKR and KPI are leadership processes for setting, communicating, and monitoring goals and results in an organization. If your organization does not set goals in this way, don't be discouraged! Reach out to those best placed to inform you on the bigger organizational goals.

6. Based on your answers to questions 1–5, who are
    the people in your organization that would benefit
    most from a design system? Focus on individual
    personas, such as a product manager, developer,
    chief marketing officer, etc. List each persona by title
    and how they'll benefit:

    • Title: How they benefit from the system...

    • Title: How they benefit from the system...

    • Title: How they benefit from the system...

Tying It All Together

You need support to make your system successful, which means that
getting buy-in before you start is essential. There are three target audiences
for a design system: the employees of the organization, the organization,
and the users of the product. Approach this in the same way you would
a design problem, by understanding each audience's unique goals and
challenges.

Each member of your organization has something to gain from a
design system. Designers will benefit from the consistency and availability
of centralized solutions. A system will buy them time, allowing them to
devote more effort to user experience, research, and exploratory work.
Engineers and product managers can gain easy access to specs and assets
and can utilize readily available solutions. Sales and marketing can use the
system to answer customer questions and demonstrate a future vision to
prospective customers.

Use both qualitative and quantitative measurements to establish the ROI of a design system for an organization. Some examples of measurable benefits are productivity, cost savings, sales, and customer satisfaction. It will be important to take baseline measurements and continue to measure results along the way.

You will have to use several methods and channels to communicate with your team and colleagues about your design system. Use the methods outlined in this chapter to further your efforts and gain buy-in within your organization.

CHAPTER 4

Design As a Language

Communication is essential in our everyday lives. It allows us to distribute knowledge, learn complex ideas, and facilitate the development of relationships. Successful communication is achieved when people share the same language. By thinking about design systems as a shared language, your organization will establish a better and more consistent means of communication. The basis of language is composed of two attributes:

- **Lexicon**: Within a language, a lexicon refers to the total number of fragments (or words) that make up that language. These fragments form the foundation of a language and can be arranged and rearranged in an infinite number of ways. When viewed in their simplest form, these fragments are meaningless. Often, it isn't until we begin using them as building blocks that we can derive meaning and effectively communicate with one another. Within a design system, these fragments make up your elements, as depicted in Figure 4-1.

© Sarrah Vesselov and Taurie Davis 2019
S. Vesselov and T. Davis, *Building Design Systems*,
https://doi.org/10.1007/978-1-4842-4514-9_4

Figure 4-1. *The distinct elements shown in this figure work together to create an interface that has different meaning than each part in isolation*

- **Grammar**: Language relies on a system of rules, known as a grammar. Without a shared understanding of the rules that govern a language, we are bound to experience misconceptions and communication breakdown. Once a grammar is established, we can focus on higher-level ideas, rather than form or structure. Within a design system, guidelines are introduced to form the grammar of our system. In other words, usage and technical guidelines help define when and how individual components should be used. Figure 4-2 shows how guidelines help to establish reusability among components.

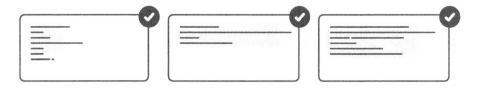

Figure 4-2. *Documented guidelines help to ensure the preceding component is consistently reused to build three separate content areas*

By thinking about design as a language system, we can create a lexicon comprised of elements and document a grammar, or series of guidelines, that govern their use.

Each language contains a different set of a lexicon and a grammar, making the language unique. In terms of a design system, guiding principles are used as the method to create a design language that is distinct to your organization. These principles enable you to build a relationship that addresses both user needs and organizational goals.

Lexicon: The Elements of Your System

Language is a system comprised of interconnecting elements that work together to aid communication. Thinking about design as a system will allow you to create the lexicon, or building blocks, that can be arranged in multiple ways to make up your product.

Depending on the state of your organization, it can be helpful to approach thinking systematically from two directions:

1. Building up elements to create larger interfaces.

2. Breaking down interfaces into their simplest elements.

Building Up Elements

If your team is starting a relatively new project, it is helpful to start with the simplest element and build your interface up from there. Start by identifying what elements are commonly used. These include various stylistic elements, such as typography and colors, as well as interactive components, such as inputs, buttons, and so on.

Once you have defined your elements, you can start to build on them, making more complex components or component groups, as shown in Figures 4-3 and 4-4.

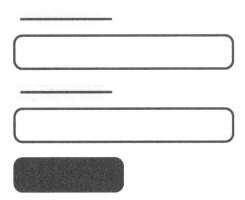

Figure 4-3. *A label, input, and button create a form*

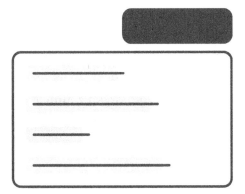

Figure 4-4. *A button with a list of anchors create a dropdown*

Component groups can then be combined to create larger interface areas, such as a navigation bar. Your navigation could comprise multiple tabs, dropdowns, and a search bar. When large groups of components come together and have a distinct set of rules, they form a region, as shown in Figure 4-5.

Figure 4-5. *Navigation region*

Note   For more information on building components, see Chapter 5.

Breaking Down Interfaces

If you have already designed interfaces for your product, it is helpful to begin by breaking down your UI and determining which aspects are repeated throughout your product or application. The most effective way of breaking down an interface is to create an inventory of the elements, components, and component groups you already use within your product.

Note   For more information on how to create an interface inventory, see Chapter 5.

How a System Helps You Scale Design

Building up and breaking down your interface are two methods of thinking about design systematically. These approaches are not sequential; they can happen at the same time. Think holistically, while also considering the individual pieces that make up the whole. Considering each piece that makes up a design will ensure that you are defining components that can be used globally across your product.

55

It is necessary to think about how your design will scale as your product grows. Not only does your team size have the potential to increase, so does the number and complexity of interactions you will have to take into account. Keeping a design system will save your team time from having to reinvent solutions. It will create cohesiveness and keep your application DRY. In turn, this creates a consistent experience that reduces friction and cognitive load for your users.

Grammar: The Guidelines of Your System

A grammar is formed when you apply formal rules to govern the behavior of your elements. This in turn creates meaning. Your design system thrives when you commit to including documentation as part of your creation process. By writing down guidelines, you are reinforcing desired behaviors and promoting consistency. Ultimately, teams are encouraged to learn your design language and use it to communicate appropriately.

When documenting new rules, think about it from multiple perspectives. Remember that the organization, your team, and your users, along with product, marketing, and engineering, all stand to benefit from the system you create. If you keep them all in mind, your language will be universal and usable by everyone.

When getting started, it can be helpful to look toward other design systems for inspiration and guidance. However, keep in mind that those organizations are solving for different goals and needs. It is important to create a system that works for your organization, rather than merely adapting the rules and guidelines that were determined for another organization.

Different Types of Guidelines

There are several types of guidelines that should be included within your design system. These include:

- **A formal definition**: A brief overview of what you are documenting. What is a button? This may seem straightforward to you, but being explicit strengthens your language and the overall understanding that your team shares.

- **Usage guidelines**: Explain the use of each component. Include behavioral rules. When should you use placeholder text within an input? How do alerts differ from toast notifications? These are questions that should be answered when reading your design system.

- **Technical guidelines**: Work closely with your engineering team to include any technical guidelines that will aid in the creation and use of a component within your product. This could include class names, as well as other options passed via data attributes or JavaScript.

- **Related components**: Link related components to help those navigating your system find what they are looking for more easily.

Remember that as components are combined to create more component groups, those component groups need documentation as well. Specific rules come out of component groups that do not exist for the individual components. For example, an input is just an input until you attach a button to it. Then it becomes a form. As a form, this component group has new guidelines and rules aside from those of its individual parts. Document the usage of buttons on their own, as well as when they are added to create a form.

When creating interfaces, some guidelines may feel organic. For example, your team may intuitively know which button to use in any specific situation. Assuming that everyone has a shared understanding of when and where to use certain components can cause teams to skip the documentation step. Take caution; skipping documentation is dangerous and leads to inconsistencies. Without clearly defined guidelines, multiple interpretations can occur. Even if the use of a component feels organic, you must define it explicitly.

Contextual Rules

Creating contextual rules may be necessary. Contextual rules occur when there is an instance that requires a deviation from the standard guidelines. Be flexible with your system but remember that creating an abundance of contextual rules or exceptions will make your system more difficult to maintain. If there is a need for an exception, ensure that you write detailed documentation explaining both the change, as well as a clear reason, so that your entire team has a shared understanding. More important, first ask yourself if an exception is truly needed or if this points to a larger consistency issue.

Our experience   A design system is not meant to be a rigid set of rules that remove creativity from the process. You are allowed to create deviations in your guidelines so long as you are intentional in your choices and document your decisions. Be strict but understand that outliers are sometimes necessary to improve your interface and user experience.

Design Principles

Every organization has a unique set of needs and goals. The ability to communicate these needs and goals through a set of principles will allow you to shape the way your organization talks about its product.

Defining Design Principles

Design principles combine organizational goals with user needs, creating the core values that aid us in making crucial design decisions. Effective design principles will align designers and build cohesiveness within your product and across teams. Additionally, design principles provide an anchor for teams to rally around. When a new member joins, your principles should be the guiding light that acquaints them with the core goals of your organization.

Successful design principles consist of phrases that provide valuable insight into both what the team is striving to accomplish and why. This means that concise, yet descriptive, principles are often more effective than single words. For example:

Minimal and efficient

vs.

Bring a sharp focus by helping customers know what matters now

Minimalism and efficiency are common traits to strive for in user experience. This often means that those words lose their power when used as principles. While it can be useful to write down keywords such as these to establish high-level goals, be sure to drill down further and determine what they mean for your organization.

Including descriptive principles in your design system will give you and your team a reference to draw upon when conflicts or uncertainty arise. The goal of your design principles is to help govern a mode of thinking for your team, setting it apart from systems used by other organizations.

A Practical Guide to Creating Your Own

Begin thinking about your own set of principles by reflecting on what your product is trying to accomplish for your users. Look to your organization's culture and consider the behaviors that you reward internally. Identify the voice you use to talk to customers and the identity you portray to users. These can provide valuable insight when determining which principles hold the most meaning for your organization.

Focus on creating three to five solid design principles that reflect the goals of your organization and the needs of your user base. Creating too many principles will make them difficult to follow and adhere to, while too few won't provide enough guidance for a wide variety of experiences.

If some principles stand out more than others, you may benefit from using a ranking system. A value hierarchy allows your team to understand which principles hold more weight. Visualizing the hierarchy by creating an ordered list, or pyramid structure, can be helpful. Alternatively, all principles may be considered equally within your organization. Both strategies are valid but should be documented clearly. If your team is experiencing conflicts often, consider reexamining the principles you've defined. Chances are that if your principles are often in conflict, then one or more may not match your goals or needs.

DEFINING YOUR DESIGN PRINCIPLES

1. **Build a team**: Start by inviting your whole team to participate. The more discussion you have as a group, the better the alignment you will achieve within your team. Include engineers and product managers as part of the conversation. Gaining their buy-in and insight from the start is vital to building your shared language.

2. **Set a clear purpose**: Ensure the team understands the objective of the meeting. The goal should be to determine which principles best align with your organizational goals and user needs. If these are unknown to you and your team, seek out key stakeholders within your organization. You should be able to produce a list of goals and needs prior to determining your design principles. Also, understand that these goals and needs may change over time.

3. **Prepare**: Ask each team member to brainstorm five to ten ideas in advance. This will make the discussion more productive, as each person will bring new ideas to the table at the start of the meeting.

4. **Discuss**: Bring physical sticky notes or use an online platform that allows you and your team to move ideas around on a board easily. This provides a way to group similar ideas and visually see which concepts stand out. Allow some time for new ideas to form and address outliers or conflicts as they come up. When in doubt, revisit your organizational goals and user needs to better map your design principles to those values.

5. **Iterate**: Goals and needs change over time. Be open to adjusting your design principles as your organization shifts. Recognize when a principle is not benefiting your team and strive to keep your principles at the forefront of your design thinking.

A Shared Language

Including other teams in the creation process of your system will lead to a better understanding of the overall language you are creating. To be fluent in a language, you must actively use it. The same can be said for your design system. The more team members you have using and contributing to it, the more cohesion your organization will experience.

Keep in mind that a design system, just like a language, can and should evolve over time. Change is a natural part of a language that allows new functions and concepts to form. As you begin to craft your own design language, be rigid with your guidelines but be open to change as your system adapts and grows.

Tying It All Together

Your design language is a vehicle for communicating. Every language consists of a lexicon and a grammar. Within your design system, elements build to components, which build to component groups, all comprising your lexicon. Your grammar is composed of the guidelines you define for each aspect of your design system, including usage and technical guidelines.

Creating your own design principles will encourage you and your team to create elements and guidelines that best serve your unique product and organization. Principles should be concise yet distinct to your organizational goals and user needs.

To strengthen your design language, involve others during the creation process. The more team members who use and contribute to your system, the more effective it will be.

CHAPTER 5

Implementing Your System

Now that we've established the "why" of a design system and learned how to think about design as a language, the next step is to begin implementation. In this section, we will start by assessing your organization, building a support system, and understanding the state of your product. You will learn how to build a predictable architecture that supports the multiple areas that make up your system. Once there is a clear foundation, you can begin designing, building, and implementing components while ensuring to clearly document decisions along the way. We've provided three case studies to help ground the discussion and provide real-world scenarios for how to implement a system based on individual needs.

Assessing Your Organization

The way you tackle your design system will largely depend on your organization. Begin by assessing the type of organization, your stakeholder buy-in, and your team size, to understand the challenges you face, as well as how to best begin implementation.

S. Vesselov and T. Davis, *Building Design Systems*,
https://doi.org/10.1007/978-1-4842-4514-9_5

Type of Organization

Is your organization a product shop or an agency? You'll want to approach your design system differently depending on whether you are building one or multiple products.

When working on one application, start by defining your layout and styles. These guidelines will establish the foundation needed for all components.

Agencies, on the other hand, often have multiple clients. Their design system has to adapt to different themes and functionality to support multiple clients and products. Start by defining or identifying the critical components that are used throughout all of your products. Create a layout system that is driven by a central set of variables. In programming, variables are used to represent a value that can change depending on the information or conditions.[1] When building interfaces, these variables include values for spacing that can be customized on a product-by-product basis. Starting from a flexible layout will give you a solid foundation that allows the freedom to customize each product and project.

You'll then work to create flexible styles that can be applied on top of your defined components to further customize and suit different needs, as demonstrated in Figure 5-1. This method, known as theming, allows you to introduce a unique visual language for each distinct brand.

---

[1]The most common method for doing this is to set up core variables, using CSS or Sass. Another method for custom theming worth noting is "design tokens." Used by Salesforce Lightning Design System, among others, design tokens are named entities that store UI attributes. They are often stored in JSON or YAML files and can be shared in nearly any format: JavaScript objects, Sass/Less/CSS variables, Sketch files, etc.

Figure 5-1. *Flexible styles can transform the same component, giving it a completely different visual language while maintaining the same foundation*

Stakeholder Buy-In

The support you have from others within your organization will play a critical role in how you build out your system. If you do not have buy-in from key stakeholders, you will have to be more strategic in approaching implementation. While helpful, it is not necessary to have stakeholder buy-in to start implementing your system. Carve out time to start defining your elements and documenting your guidelines as a first step. Keep track of how these improvements are helping you work faster and smarter to build the business case. As these become more concrete, the perceived value of your system will grow over time, and the business case will be more evident to the organization.

Note   For more information on how to gain stakeholder buy-in, review Chapter 3.

Team Size

A small team typically struggles to find the necessary time to build out a fully functioning system, while a large organization may grapple with getting ahead of the inconsistencies that have built up over the years. The problems you experience will vary, depending on the size of the team. Remain aware of the challenges your organization is facing and be prepared to come up with a game plan to address these problems at the start of implementation.

Review the case studies at the end of this chapter for real-world insight into how your type of organization, stakeholder buy-in, and team size can all affect your design system.

Gathering a Support System

Once you've assessed your organization, begin to gather support from co-workers. Some organizations are lucky enough to form dedicated design system teams that comprise designers, engineers, and product managers. However, this is relatively uncommon when first beginning. It is more likely that you will start on your own, with the help of a few co-workers you may have to recruit.

Clearly articulate what a design system is when talking with your peers. One common misconception is that a design system is solely a place to house the visual aspect of each component. To address this misconception, explain that a design system encompasses all areas of your platform: from design principles and usability guidelines, to live component examples, and technical rules.

Build enthusiasm among those who show interest in learning more about your effort. These will be your most reliable allies throughout the process. If you don't have a technical background, it is crucial to form a relationship with the members of your team who can assist with the technical implementation. Without them, you will struggle to make headway on completing your design system.

Over the course of implementation, you will need a team that can:

- Research best practices.

- Make an interface inventory.

- Design and define your layout, styles, and components.

- Document guidelines.

- Review documentation.

- Build and implement components.

- Iterate and refine.

- Evangelize your efforts across your organization.

Assessing Your Product

Creating systematic design requires a structured approach. If you jump straight into creating new components for your product without first understanding the current state of your interface, you will fall into the trap of continuously redesigning the same components. Begin by understanding where your problem areas are in order to create a system that brings focus and efficiency.

Utilize an Interface Inventory

Inconsistencies within your product can lead to confusing experiences for your users. To help understand the current state of your product or application, create an interface inventory. An inventory will surface inconsistencies and lay the groundwork for correcting them.

Note   If your product is brand new, you may choose to forgo creating an interface inventory at this time.

To begin, capture and record all of the elements and components used within your UI. The easiest way to do this is to screenshot each one. You don't need to log every instance, simply document each unique design.

Include typography, inputs, radios, buttons, etc. Be meticulous. Every individual element and component used throughout your product should be recorded. Navigate page by page until you feel confident that you have grabbed each one.

From here, you can begin categorizing. Group duplicates together and look for inconsistencies, as shown in Figure 5-2.

Figure 5-2. *An interface inventory showing icon inconsistencies*

Use your interface inventory as a jumping-off point. Now that you have everything recorded, you'll be able to use this to start working toward a comprehensive component library. Knowing the current state of your product will allow you to successfully break down your design system into intuitive categories.

Creating a Predictable Architecture

How you organize your system is crucial to the success of your design system. Breaking your system down into predictable categories will keep your content easily discoverable. Remain open to adjusting the architecture as you build out and expand on your system.

Categorizing to Improve Discoverability

A successful design system will contain multiple parts. As mentioned earlier in Chapter 2, you can break down your design system into the following six interlocking areas:

> **Layout**: Defined measures that make up your spacing and grid system.
>
> **Styles**: Core aspects of your visual language. These include colors, iconography, and typography.
>
> **Components**: Core elements of an interface. These include buttons and form fields.
>
> **Regions**: Overarching design paradigms, such as navigation or search.
>
> **Content**: Information regarding the voice and tone, as well as punctuation guidelines. Content can also include terminology if your product has a specific vocabulary.
>
> **Usability**: Rules that define accessibility and internationalization.

Breaking your system down into sections will provide a sense of organization, making it easier to find the information required to complete a specific task.

Using the preceding six categories as a base, begin to piece together the structure for your system. Your system should consider all areas, but they will vary in size depending on your organization. Don't get stuck on conforming to a set of categories or rules that don't work for your organizational goals or user needs. Categories will help to communicate different areas of focus, but keep in mind that your design language needs room to grow and evolve over time.

Card Sorting

As your design system expands, you may not always be sure where specific content should live. When this happens, utilize a card-sorting technique to determine what should be grouped together. You may find that you need to add a new category, or change a category name, to fit new content.

How to Perform a Card Sort

There are many tools available to assist with creating a card sort, but all you really need are pen and paper. The primary objective is to determine how people categorize the information in your system to build a predictable architecture.

1. If you've already begun creating your design system, start by capturing the different parts that make up your system. Include any new components or guidelines you are looking to add. Use your interface inventory to incorporate components you have identified. Drag-and-drop interactions, common terms, and filters are perfect examples of what you may be looking to categorize.

Note   You will want to limit the number of cards you create to reduce fatigue during the study. This may mean that not all elements or guidelines are captured in your research. Aim to be broad enough so that you can use the findings to categorize cards that didn't make it into the test. Alternatively, if you don't have enough cards to test, it will be difficult for users to find parallels between them. Try to keep your number of cards between 30 and 50.

---

2. Recruit seven to ten participants to take part in your card sort.

3. For each participant, mix up the order of your cards and allow them to organize the content into any categories they choose. Give the participant the opportunity to write their own category names. This will give you more insight into how they would structure and define the content.

4. After every participant has finished their sorting, analyze how often the same cards were grouped together, as well as how often the same categories were created.

5. Use your analysis to tweak the information architecture of your system as needed.

Layout

A foundational aspect included in your system is the layout, which includes guidelines for both your spacing and grid. These provide a solid base from which you can create components and build interfaces.

Remember: If you are creating a system for multiple products, consider creating a series of variables that allow you to customize your layout for each one.

Spacing

A series of spacing increments will create the foundation for the padding and margin used within your product. Figure 5-3 shows how padding and margin are applied to a series of buttons to make up the spacing.

Padding   ▒ Margin

Figure 5-3. *Padding is used to add space between the text and borders of the buttons, while margin makes up the space between components*

Create a spacing system that uses a set series of increments for defining padding and margin. Specify a starting number from which your spacing will derive. A starting number of eight is often used for spacing systems because it is scaled easily to different resolutions, making it ideal for the growing number of devices that are out there today. Also, a base of eight provides a variety of increments when used within a mathematical progression without overwhelming designers with choices. This is demonstrated in Figure 5-4. As an alternative, use a geometric progression to limit the number of options further while still allowing for visually appealing interfaces. Regardless of the progression you choose, be deliberate in your decision.

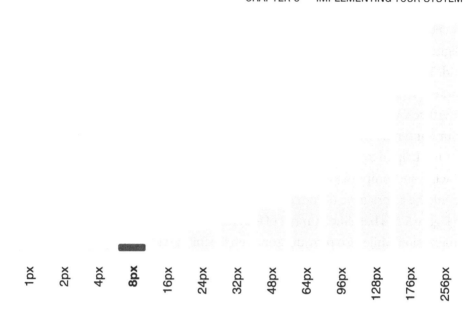

Figure 5-4. *A spacing system using a mathematical progression with a starting base of 8px*

In the end, you will have to determine the most appropriate starting number for your needs, as well as the increments to use across your product.

Grid

There are multiple types of grids, most commonly column and baseline grids. Column grids are regularly used within web development to separate discontinuous content. Equal spacing between columns keeps content divided uniformly, allowing users to digest information quickly. Column grids can also be rearranged to accommodate different screen sizes, making them ideal for implementing a responsive design. While column grids are useful in many layouts, they may not always be appropriate in others. A complex web app may require more flexibility than column grids allow. High-density information, for example, would benefit from implementing a strict measurement system that could be used in place of, or in addition to, column grids.

Further, utilizing a baseline grid will keep your units horizontally aligned to one another. Baseline grids align all of your text to a horizontal grid. The x-height[2] of each letter is anchored onto this grid, keeping content legible and reducing the guesswork when building out new user interfaces. With consistent spacing, you can ensure that the hierarchy of your content is well-defined and easy to determine.

It is helpful to choose a baseline number that provides flexibility when spacing out components while also creating legible line-heights. Your baseline should be a derivative of your spacing system. In the spacing example shown in Figure 5-5, a baseline number of four aligns with your mathematical progression while also providing enough flexibility within your designs.

Figure 5-5. *Components placed on a baseline grid of 4px*

Styles

Your styles make up your visual language and include typography, colors, and icons. As you define these elements, be sure to reference the design principles you created for your organization. This will help to align your overall visual language with the design language you are crafting.

If you are working with one product, you only need to define your styles once. However, if you are building a system for multiple products

---

[2]*"x-height"* refers to the height of a lower-case *x*. In typography, the x-height represents the distance between the baseline and the midline of lower case letters for a given typeface.

or clients, you will need to create a theming system that allows you to customize the visual language of each unique product.

Creating a Typographic System

Typography that functions well, conforms to user needs, and aligns with your baseline grid can be a challenge to get right. To ensure that your typography aligns with your baseline grid and has readable line-heights, we have found that it is useful to break down your typography into two categories: UI typography and long-form typography.

UI typography makes up the text used within your UI components, such as button text, input labels, or dropdown options. To ensure that your elements align to your baseline grid, the line-height of your UI typography should strictly align to a multiple of the starting number chosen in your layout rules. This is shown in Figure 5-6.

16px [**Label copy**   ] 4px

                              ] 8px
32px [Placeholder   ] 16px
                              ] 8px

16px [Help text   ] 4px

Figure 5-6. *The UI typography within the input box uses a line-height of 16px. This is a multiple of the starting unit 8, chosen in the illustrated spacing system*

In many cases, the line-height for UI typography can feel crowded when applied to larger bodies of text. In these instances, create a system for long-form typography that uses improved line-heights for better readability, as demonstrated in Figures 5-7 and 5-8. If your product includes any form of descriptive text, you should consider whether creating a separate long-form typography system would benefit your users.

When using typography within your UI, you want to use a line height that matches your base measurement number. However, this means that wrapped text will have poor readability due to it's small line height.

To fix this, you can create a system to use for long-form text. This provides the flexibility you need to create text styles that have improved line heights for readability.

Figure 5-7. *Line-heights for UI typography are too small for readable text when used for long-form text*

UI Heading 1
UI Heading 2
UI Heading 3
UI Heading 4
UI Label

Long-form Heading 01
Long-form Heading 02
Long-form Heading 03
Long-form Heading 04
Long-form paragraph

Figure 5-8. *UI typography vs. long-form typography*

Aligning your typography with your baseline grid and measurement system is one of the more frustrating parts to get right. It can take a lot of trial and error. Take time to experiment. Nailing down a typographic system that aligns with your layout makes the remainder of your visual decisions a breeze.

An Accessible Color System

Colors are an important consideration when determining the aesthetic of your product or projects. Because they do not affect layout or functionality, your color palette can be iterated freely. This makes your color system an easy first choice if you are struggling with where to begin once you start technical implementation.

As you build or refine your color system, keep accessibility at the forefront of your mind. Colors play a huge role in calling attention to individual UI elements, but a lack of contrast between colors can quickly make your application difficult to use by users with visual impairments. Depending on your organization, you may have to support a higher level of contrast, as defined by the Web Content Accessibility Guidelines (WCAG). For example, organizations that operate internationally will encounter a higher accessibility threshold due to stricter laws in some countries. Figure 5-9 shows different color combinations with their WCAG rating.

Contrast ratio: 21:1	Contrast ratio: 7:1	Contrast ratio: 4:7	Contrast ratio: 2:9
Normal text	Normal text	Normal text	Normal text
✓ AA	✓ AA	✓ AA	✘ AA
✓ AAA	✓ AAA	✘ AAA	✘ AAA
Large text	Large text	Large text	Large text
✓ AA	✓ AA	✓ AA	✘ AA
✓ AAA	✓ AAA	✓ AAA	✘ AAA

Figure 5-9. *Color combinations and their corresponding rating, according to the WCAG*

As shown in Figure 5-10, you may choose to create a color system that includes palettes for each primary color. These palettes include shade variations, such as secondary and tertiary options. Like other areas of your system, the more options you add, the more flexibility you will have. Keep in mind that this flexibility can bring inconsistencies while also making documentation more challenging to manage.

Figure 5-10. *A series of shades that make up a palette. This provides flexibility and the ability to define primary, secondary, and tertiary options.*

Our experience   If you choose to create an expansive color system, implement color priorities to reduce your decision making during the design process. You can achieve color priorities by creating a system similar to font weights. Assign your colors a numbered value that corresponds to the hierarchy in which they should be used.

Uniform Iconography

Not all products will require their own set of icons. You can take advantage of multiple open source icon fonts. However, one primary benefit of creating your own set of icons is the ability to align them with your distinct visual language. If you are creating your own icon set, remember to document your process thoroughly. Establish an icon grid and core shapes in order to maintain proportions and visual consistency across icons. The rest of your team should understand the structure that makes up your icons, as well as how to export and include them within your application. If necessary, get the help of your engineering team to create an icon viewer that allows your organization to search for existing icons quickly. For ease of use, include a way to copy the source code or download a vector version.

Components

As you begin to design and define components, look back at what was included within your interface inventory. Establish a structure that mimics the way components will be implemented. A systematic approach will bring your design and engineering teams closer together while ensuring that components stay DRY and reusable.

Creating a Component Library

Building a component library will help your design team to visually see how layout and style guidelines apply to each component. Often, your component library will start within a design tool, but it can also be created directly in code.

You can use your component library as a playground when first determining your primary set of guidelines. Remember to think about your specific product and start by creating the components that are most relevant to your needs.

Review your inventory and choose the ten most widely used components to get started. This most often will mean starting with the basic components that make up your interface: buttons, inputs, labels, tool tips, etc. Beginning with these will create a solid foundation on which to build more complex component groups as you work through your interface inventory.

Tooling

There are many different tools you can use throughout the creation process. This can include design software, front-end frameworks, and UI development environments.

- **Design software**: Tools, such as Sketch or Figma, give your design team the flexibility to play with applying different guidelines to your components.

- **Front-end frameworks**: Many front-end teams use frameworks as a base for their component structure that can then be easily modified to fit unique styles. Bootstrap and Foundation are common web frameworks used by many teams.

- **UI development environments**: Your team may also choose to use an interactive UI development environment, such as Storybook. Tools like these allow developers to build components in an isolated setting, providing a way to easily test each component independently of your product.

Choosing tools can be an arduous task, especially considering the number of options available for designers and engineers today. It is easy to get caught up in the latest tool, turning progress into tool churn.

Tools are always evolving, but it's important to keep in mind that constant change may slow progress. Evaluate your tools carefully and decide what is best for your team at this moment. Don't get caught up in a niche toolset that may disappear in a few months. Look at numerous aspects, such as performance, scalability, and reliability. The tools and technologies you use to create your library are meant to help your team create your design system, not act as the solution.

Building Components

In Chapter 4, we talked about how to build up elements to create components, component groups, and regions. This systematic structure is important to keep in mind throughout the process of building your component library. Thinking about your interface in this way will mimic the way in which your product is built by your engineering team.

There are many other methodologies that exist to help structure design in a systematic way. You may choose whichever methodology works for you, so long as you are thinking about your interface as building blocks. If this is a new concept for you, be sure to bring in engineers early and get their perspective often. Doing so will strengthen your design language and propel implementation.

Remember: All your components should adhere to the rules you have previously defined in other sections. If you are working for an agency and do not yet have a set of flexible styles, create a series of components with base styles that you can apply themes to later.

Regions

Your system needs a place for documentation related to larger paradigms that go beyond your components. These areas are often reused throughout your product and have specific guidelines that relate to the region as a whole.

For example, you may choose to classify a search bar as a component. However, if search plays a primary role within your product, has many interactions, and is reused often, consider categorizing search as a region. By setting it apart from an individual component, you recognize that the region has guidelines that are made up of more than its building blocks.

Regions provide the space to expand on interactions specific to your product. For example, if your application has different user permissions, you can include guidelines related to how they affect your interface and user experience. You may choose to add rules for logged-in vs. logged-out users. Regions also typically consist of rules that apply to your navigation structure, such as guidelines for global and contextual navigation or a complex hierarchical structure. What you decide to include as a region will largely depend on what product you are building.

Content

Like regions, your content section will rely on the needs of your product. This is a place for you to capture the voice and tone you want to portray in your application. Collaborate with marketing to create a shared writing style and include useful terminology that is specific to your organization.

If you are working for an agency, this section will provide the space needed to create guidelines that help propel new projects. If your clients are similar, you can create a standardized voice to reference across projects. However, if your clients are varied, this section will act as a reference point for different scenarios. Create guidelines that are useful for your agency to consider when taking on new clients. This could include the voice you want to portray when working with a client who caters to children vs. one who works primarily with mortgage brokers. One will be fun and friendly, while the other will be more professional. Every product is unique, so the documentation you write in this section should be solely guidelines to reference and help get you started on new projects.

Usability

How usable your product is will define its success. Users should be able to familiarize themselves with your user interface quickly and without too much prompting. They should be able to achieve their objectives directly and with as little friction as possible. Upon returning to your product, they should be able to recall how to navigate and perform familiar actions. When building out your design system, include guidelines that will improve the usability of your product. Two common usability concerns include accessibility and internationalization.

Accessibility

Regardless of whether you are working for a product shop or an agency, your design system should include accessibility guidelines. If you haven't considered accessibility concerns, this is the perfect time to introduce this way of thinking into your organization.

There are various levels of accessibility, such as visual, hearing, and cognitive impairments, as well as motor disabilities. Keeping these at the forefront of your mind while designing will improve the overall experience for your users.

Depending on your audience, you will have to consider all accessibility concerns and document the most appropriate action for your organization to take. Should your product work with screen readers? Do your colors pass WCAG contrast ratio standards? Do your touch points on mobile have large enough targets? Is your font readable? In nearly all circumstances, your design system should take into account how your product will support these usability concerns.

To show your commitment to accessibility, include a statement of compliance. This statement should include your commitment to maintaining an accessible product, as well as the level of compliance to which you aim to conform. It is important to create guidelines for your individual product. It is not always necessary to conform to all levels of compliance. Understand your user needs and create a statement of compliance that functions well for your intended audience.

Our experience   The Information Technology Industry (ITI) Council produces a Voluntary Product Accessibility Template (VPAT) that you can use to assess the compliance of your product. While this document may be overwhelming at first, it is invaluable in learning the leading accessibility standards while also showcasing where your product can improve.

Internationalization

If you are delivering content to users around the world, internationalization is something you will have to account for and document. Supporting multiple languages will mean including translation mechanisms, changes in word alignment (right to left vs. left to right), as well as line-height and letter-spacing changes. Cultural differences should also be accounted for. Language and imagery should be tailored to best suit the culture of the region it is being delivered to.

Technical Implementation

Defining, designing, and implementing your system can happen simultaneously. Begin by defining your layout, styles, and components. As you start to feel confident in your new guidelines, work closely with front-end engineers to begin implementing them in your design system. As you work in parallel, issues will surface. Working together will allow you to fix unexpected problems earlier in the process.

If you created your component library using design software, use this as a tool to help communicate. Once you have begun to build your system using live code, this will become the primary reference for your organization. Involve product, design, and engineering in the decision making and understand that changes and additions along the way are inevitable.

A Single Source of Truth

One of the most difficult challenges teams face is the technical implementation of their design system. Think about your system as a dependency for your product; it should be the single source of truth that manages the state of your components. The components within your design system should all utilize the same code that make up the building blocks of your product.

To build your components, you and your engineering team will use a series of programming tools to implement the markup (HTML), styling (CSS), and functionality (JavaScript) that you've defined in your guidelines.[3] Think of these programming tools as associated assets that are consumed by both your design system and your product. When used in this way, you are ensuring that your design system is the single source of truth for your product.

It is common for edge cases to become apparent when your designs are applied to real-world scenarios. Take the necessary time to fix problems and iterate along the way. As you continue to build and implement the components within your system, you will want to manage revisions that are made over time. This workflow, known as version control,[4] allows you to compare old versions of your components with new changes. In the event of a mistake, you can reference previous decisions or even revert to older versions. Using a version control system ultimately ensures your entire team knows which version of your component is most recent and up-to-date.

Incremental Implementation

Unless you are starting with a brand-new application, you will want to introduce changes into your product incrementally. When replacing old components, there are two common methods:

- Replace one element throughout the entire product,

- Replace elements page by page.

---

[3]HTML, CSS, and JavaScript are common languages used for web applications. If you are building a design system for mobile products, the technologies used will vary.

[4]The most common system used for version control is Git. It is free and open source. To learn more about how to use Git to manage your workflow, check out `https://git-scm.com/`.

Replacing a component throughout your entire product is excellent for maintaining consistency. However, if you have a large application, this method can be overwhelming. Components affect other components, and if you are changing your entire typography or spacing system, this will have a cascading effect. On the other hand, replacing elements one page at a time can hinder the user experience. You don't want to confuse users by having multiple interactions for the same component.

Which method you choose will depend on how large your product is, how much time your team can dedicate towards implementing these changes, and the complexity of your product. Most often, it will be more realistic to use a combination of both methods. For example, implement your typography system page by page. While you work on implementing your typography across your product, you can also replace a simple component, such as inputs, all at once.

Our experience   You won't be able to implement all your components immediately. If you already have a product built, don't waste time documenting guidelines for components you are going to replace. Instead, spend your energy on creating rules for new components you've defined in your component library. While this means that your design system will reference guidelines that are not implemented, it will create a single source of truth for what your product should be utilizing.

Documentation

As we discussed in Chapter 4, there are many guidelines that must be documented. These guidelines, as well as live code examples, will make up the primary documentation for your design system.

Provide clearly defined rules for how each component will be used. Readers should be able to answer the what, when, where, and why of each component you have documented. You will need to include any implementation rules that assist in using your components. This means including class names and code snippets. Providing live code examples will tie together usage guidelines with the technical rules, providing a visual representation of how the component should look and function. Avoid including static images that can easily become out of date over time.

As you implement your system iteratively, it is beneficial to call out the state of each component. Create a page that shows each component status. Include whether it is upcoming, in progress, or stable and ready for use. Tag components as "new" if they've been recently added to your design system. Providing visibility into the status of each component gives your team a clear overview of the progress being made to your system.

Establish a System That Self-Documents

Writing documentation is a challenge, and keeping documentation up to date is even tougher. By following the recommendations in this chapter, you will have created a structure that utilizes the same component for both your design system and your product. When a change is made to a component, the effect will be seen in both places. This keeps your components up to date without having to manually make changes. Change the code in one place, and your design system will update along with your product.

Searchability

You can vastly improve the usability of your design system by including a way for your team to search through documentation. Finding the piece of documentation that you need can be difficult and time-consuming. Make it easier for your organization to use the documentation that you have worked so hard on by adding the ability to search the content you have created.

Tying It All Together

To start implementing your design system, you must first assess your organization. Come to understand how your type of organization will affect the decisions you must make when building your system. Learn whether you have stakeholder buy-in or if this is something you will have to develop over time. Recruit peers who show an interest in learning more and participating in the creation of your design system.

While you build a support network, assess the state of your current product. Utilize an interface inventory if your product is already underway. Begin to break down your product into the following six areas: layout, styles, components, regions, content, and usability. These categories will keep your design system organized, but don't be afraid to create your own. Use a card-sorting technique to better understand how to group different information within your system.

Define a set of layout guidelines and styles that can be applied to your components. If you are working with multiple products, create flexible styles that allow you to theme your system based on each brand's unique visual language. Determine which regions are essential to document and include unique content rules, such as voice and tone. Last, ensure that usability is at the forefront of your mind. Document accessibility guidelines and include internationalization rules if that is relevant to your organization.

Work closely with your engineering team to make your design system the single source of truth for your organization. Implement a version control system that allows your team to reference previous iterations of your components. Make documentation a part of your creative process, and you will ensure that your system remains useful to your entire organization.

Case Studies

On the following pages, you will find examples of the different scenarios you may experience. Bear in mind that there are countless combinations, and every organization is unique. Use the following case studies as a starting point toward understanding the unique challenges your organization is facing and how your team can navigate those during the beginning of your process.

A SINGLE PRODUCT WITH A LARGE TEAM

Organization Type

You work for a quickly growing organization that ships new features to users regularly. There are tight deadlines, and you ship fast, which sometimes means the user experience is not what you would like it to be. Engineers work closely with designers to ensure that you ship the best first iteration in the time allotted. The executive team doesn't quite see the benefit of a design system. However, as long as you continue to ship product, it doesn't get in the way of creating one.

Team Description

You are on a large team that consists of a half-dozen designers and roughly 30 front-end engineers. The product designers were hired after the application had begun to be implemented. All designers have a decent grasp of their visual language, even though it has never been deliberately defined.

Challenges

There are numerous inconsistencies throughout the application that have grown over the years. You are aware of them but can't quite seem to get ahead.

Where to Begin

Begin by documenting what you already know intuitively. You may have typography already established but not yet defined. Write down everything that is widely known to create your foundation. Then, begin to use this documentation to surface inconsistencies in your components. Don't forget to utilize an interface inventory! Work component-by-component to integrate any documented changes into your product.

The Initial Benefit of a Design System

Over time, inconsistencies will begin to disappear as you start to document and implement your system.

AN AGENCY WITH A MEDIUM TEAM

Organization Type

You work for an agency that brings in new clients throughout the year. Most projects are similar, and you are typically working on multiple projects at the same time. You move around from project-to-project as organizational needs shift and new clients come on board. Stakeholders are not concerned with a design system because they do not see how it could help clients.

Team Description

You are part of a team with three designers and ten front-end engineers. The first UX designer was hired shortly after the engineers came on board. Client demand increased, so two more designers were hired. As a team of three, you started a team component library, to keep components consistent throughout your design tool. This made it easier to reuse components from client-to-client. However, it is common for designers to add new components without updating or cleaning up old ones, and this has made upkeep difficult. The library is in jeopardy of being abandoned.

Challenges

The team library is not scaling with the team. It is becoming unwieldy and not useful. You aren't sure how to keep it up to date as you continue to work on new projects.

Where to Begin

Begin by creating an interface inventory for your past three projects. This will help establish the primary components you use across projects. With a component library already started, you are in an excellent position to update your existing files using strict rules. After you have a clear inventory to work from, create base components that you can apply different styles to depending on the client. Getting your system implemented will be imperative since updating styles for each product will be much easier when you have theming in place.

The Initial Benefit of a Design System

Starting your design system will increase productivity. It will also close gaps within your team and free up time spent on dealing with old, outdated design files from dead projects.

A SINGLE PRODUCT WITH A SMALL TEAM

Organization Type

You work for a small startup that is just getting off the ground. This is your first job as a user-experience designer, and you are learning the ropes as quickly as you can. Your boss is invested in your learning but is more focused on both business and product.

Team Description

You are a team of one designer and four engineers. The team was hired around the same time, at the start of the project. Because you are the sole designer, there are not many inconsistencies in the product. However, you are not in constant communication with the engineers, and therefore, not all your designs translate as expected during the implementation phase.

Challenges

With limited development background, your designs may not always come out as expected. You struggle to speak in the same language as your engineering team.

Where to Begin

Begin by working closely with your front-end team to understand all the components being used within your product. Sit down with them and make a list of the top-ten components used and start applying a set of defined styles to them. Work to shape a shared design language that both you and your front-end team will understand.

The Initial Benefit of a Design System

As your design system begins to form, you will start to have more power over the experiences you are creating. You'll gain a better understanding of implementation limitations and be more adept at designing experiences that translate well to code. As the implemented design becomes more predictable and familiar to you, the overall user experience will improve as well.

CHAPTER 6

Measure and Maintain

Design systems require continuous effort. Even as you are writing design guidelines and working with engineering to implement your components, there will be revisions and improvements to be made along the way. Focus on the following key areas as you continue to grow your design system: measuring the effectiveness, understanding how to scale with your organization and product, and learning how to iterate over time.

Measuring Effectiveness

Your design system is only as effective as it is useful. To make sure it is achieving results, you'll have to make plans to measure your design system's effectiveness objectively.

Building out a design system is hard work. It can be easy to feel discouraged and wonder if your efforts are paying off. Seeing data that shows its effectiveness will help keep the team's momentum going. If the data you collect indicates that the system is not making the difference you anticipated, you can take steps to make the necessary course corrections.

Stakeholders will also want reassurance that your system is working. Design systems can increase speed and agility for your team, reduce technical debt, and improve the user experience. Focus your measurement efforts on the items listed in the business case you created in Chapter 3. Gather baseline data before introducing your system and check in at critical points along the way.

© Sarrah Vesselov and Taurie Davis 2019
S. Vesselov and T. Davis, *Building Design Systems*,
https://doi.org/10.1007/978-1-4842-4514-9_6

When communicating with the executive team and members of management, it can be helpful to frame results in terms of the cost savings and profit. How has your system saved the company time and money? How has it positively affected the user experience in a way that increased customer retention and sales?

Note   To learn more about making the business case for your design system, review Chapter 3.

Gathering Data Through Goal-Setting

Establishing Objective and Key Results (OKRs) for your design system can be a helpful way to track results. Google introduced OKRs as a tool to track alignment and progress toward shared, measurable goals. They consist of an objective, what you want to achieve, and key results, the set of outcomes that signal you have met your goal.[1] Here are a few OKR examples to illustrate how this can work in tracking your system's effectiveness:

> **Objective**: Reduce UX cycle time to increase speed to market.
>
> - **Key Result**: Define the road map for getting all "priority one" user experience components into the system (these could be core elements, such as typography, color, etc., or high-priority product features).
>
> - **Key Result**: Publish eight finalized guidelines to the system each month.
>
> - **Key Result**: Reduce UX review time spent on code changes by 50%.

---

[1]Christina Wodtke, *Introduction to OKRs*, (Sebastopol, CA: O'Reilly Media, Inc., 2016).

Objective: Accessibility is built into everything we do.

- **Key Result**: 100% of new components ship with accessibility standards checklist met.

- **Key Result**: By the end of three months, all existing components will be updated to meet accessibility standards.

Objective: The design system is an organization-wide resource.

- **Key Result**: Increase membership of non-design team members in the design system team chat[2] channel by ten members each month.

- **Key Result**: Increase design system contributions by five non-design team members each month.

Whether your organization uses OKRs or some other way to measure goals, use them to your advantage. There are many ways to measure and demonstrate how useful your design system is for your organization and your user base. Focus on creating measurable goals that allow you to track results related to your business case. This can include:

- Maximized adoption within a certain time period.

- Commitment to adopt.

- Reduced development times and increased time to market.

- Reduced technical debt and bugs.

- Improved user experience.

- Increased collaboration among teams.

---

[2]If your organization uses a chat tool, create a channel dedicated to your design system. Examples of popular team chat tools include Slack, Hipchat, and Microsoft Teams.

Gathering Data Through Surveys

Surveys are another way to measure how useful your design system is for your organization, especially if you don't have access to analytics or usage data. Create a survey to send to your fellow colleagues that helps you understand the state of your system, what you may need to change, and what can be added to make your system more effective and efficient.

When creating your survey, be sure to include questions that will capture how much time is being spent on team members inquiring about styling or usage guidelines. Over time, these guidelines will be captured within your system, allowing everyone to be more autonomous. You can also ask UX designers how much time they are spending answering style or usage questions vs. brainstorming solutions to problems.

Send the survey when you first start the process of creating your design system, as well as after you have made significant progress. By sending out the survey in regular intervals, you can measure how effective your system is compared to the previously sent survey. Overall, you will see that there is less time spent on discussions that revolve around styling and usage as your design system becomes easier to navigate, with robust and up-to-date guidelines. With this information, you can keep the momentum going and continue to gain buy-in from key stakeholders.

Survey Template

Below is a sample survey to utilize within your team. Customize the questions and answers to better suit your individual organization.

TEAM MEMBER SURVEY

Which team are you a member of?

- Front-end

- Back-end

- Product

- Marketing

- Support

- Sales

- Other

How often do you ask a UX designer or front-end engineer for help regarding the styling of a component?

- 0–1 time a cycle

- 2–4 times a cycle

- 5–7 times a cycle

- 8+ times a cycle

How often do you ask a UX designer or front-end engineer for help regarding the usage of a component?

- 0–1 time a cycle

- 2–4 times a cycle

- 5–7 times a cycle

- 8+ times a cycle

On average, how long does it take to get the assistance you need regarding the usage or styling of a component?

- I don't have to ask for help with usage or style guidelines.

- Under an hour

- 1–3 hours

- 4–8 hours

- 1 day

- 2+ days

How often are you able to work on a UI bug or improvement without UX assistance or review?

- Frequently (most problems)

- Sometimes (some problems)

- Rarely (once in a while)

- Never

- Other [text field]

How often do you visit the design system to answer a question regarding a component?

- Frequently (most questions)

- Sometimes (some questions)

- Rarely (very few questions)

- Never

- Other [text field]

If you do not utilize the design system as a resource, tell us why.

- It doesn't have what I'm looking for.

- Guidelines are out of date.

- It's difficult to navigate.

- I didn't know there was a design system.

- Other [text field]

On average, are you able to find the information you are looking for within the design system?

- Yes

- No

What can we add to the design system that would help improve your process?

- [Open-ended question]

It can also be useful to create a similar survey that is directed toward members of your design team. This will give you specific feedback regarding their time spent, as well as their perception of the usefulness of the design system. Remember to take one of the surveys yourself as well!

UX MEMBER SURVEY

How often are you asked to help clarify the styling of a component?

- 0–3 times a cycle

- 4–6 times a cycle

- 7–9 times a cycle

- 10+ times a cycle

How often are you asked to help clarify the usage of a component?

- 0–3 times a cycle

- 4–6 times a cycle

- 7–9 times a cycle

- 10+ times a cycle

How much time do you spend responding to questions regarding the styling or usage of a component?

- Less than 25% per week

- 26–50% per week

- 51–75% per week

- 76%+ per week

How much time do you spend responding to questions or doing reviews for new features?

- Less than 25% per week

- 26–50% per week

- 51–75% per week

- 76%+ per week

How much time do you spend writing documentation?

- Less than 25% per week

- 26–50% per week

- 51–75% per week

- 76%+ per week

How much time do you spend brainstorming and creating solutions to new problems?

- Less than 25% per week

- 26–50% per week

- 51–75% per week

- 76%+ per week

How often do you reference the design system when working on design related tasks?

- Frequently (most problems)

- Sometimes (some problems)

- Rarely (very few problems)

- Never

- Other [text field]

How often do you reference the design system when answering a user-experience related question?

- Frequently (most questions)

- Sometimes (some questions)

- Rarely (very few questions)

- Never

- Other [text field]

Overall, how useful is the current design system to you in your work?

- Very useful

- Somewhat useful

- Not very useful

- Not useful at all

What makes the design system useful or not useful to you?

- [Open ended question]

Measuring the effectiveness of your design system will be crucial to its success. Frame the context of your data in terms of who you are communicating with. Design and development managers will care about how the design system helps their teams function internally while an executive will care about time and money. Tell an effective story and be able to defend your business case, enabling you to continue on the path of building an effective design system.

Maintaining Your System in the Face of Growth

As you work on your design system, it is inevitable that your organization and product will experience change. This change comes in many forms: growth, reorganization, new product focus—the list goes on and on. Continuous, and sometimes rapid, growth presents both opportunity and risk for your design system.

Opportunities

- The ability to work on initiatives for which you previously lacked resources.

- The capacity to create a team dedicated to the design system.

- Enriched user experiences (depth).

- The opportunity to add additional features the product is lacking (breadth).

Risks

- Loss of culture and morale as too many people are added too fast.

- Increased UX debt as new team members fail to understand or use the design system. UX debt could also increase if UX hiring lags behind engineering or product.

- The inability to sufficiently support the design system due to time spent onboarding new team members.

There are many outside influences and factors that can affect the growth and progress of your design system. Don't allow yourself to get bogged down by what could happen. Learn to recognize the opportunities and risks and use them to your advantage.

Organizational Growth

Organizations are not static; they grow and change over time. When an organization enters a high-growth phase, it is both exciting and stressful. Organizations hire more employees when there is the opportunity to grow the product and its footprint within the market. This is a good sign that the organization is healthy and headed in the right direction. It also means onboarding new employees, adding additional managers, and making sure processes support the growth and change. To maintain and continue to grow your design system, you will have to make sure every new member becomes familiar with it.

Onboard new designers properly. Ensure that every new designer on the team gets proper instruction on how to use and contribute to your system.

Utilize organizational announcements to educate other departments. It isn't enough to have a design system. You will have to share, socialize, and evangelize it continually. Reach out to new product managers and developers. Conduct AMAs (Ask Me Anythings) or webinars for internal employees.

Product Growth

Products are not static, either. As the product matures, features are added and taken away. The visual design and user experience of the product undergo constant iteration as user feedback comes in and new designers add new insights. A side effect of these changes is UX debt. UX debt refers to the inconsistencies that accumulate and have a negative impact on user experience. These can include differences between styles you have documented and those found in the product, as well as misuse of components across features.

Tackling UX Debt

UX debt creeps in when the solutions and standards in your design system have not yet been implemented into the product. These lingering discrepancies can feel particularly painful to your team. Just like developing your design system, addressing UX debt will be a continuous process.

Accounting for UX debt is important to maintaining and growing your system. Discrepancies can lead to confusion and require more communication between engineering and design to ensure that things are being implemented correctly. Without a reliable single source of truth, the speed and efficiency of the engineers and designers working on the product will be greatly affected.

Incremental implementation. It is tempting to try and fix existing problems all at once. This can lead to long, drawn-out debates and little to no progress. You may need to implement newly defined styles one feature at a time. Create a road map for these changes and communicate it across the organization.

Consistency. Give your designers ownership of the system and hold them accountable. Try and schedule a certain number of improvements for each sprint. These could be UX debt issues already in the product or corrections and additions to the design system itself.

Collaboration. Work alongside product management and engineering to tackle existing UX issues. This isn't just a problem for the design team, this is an organizational problem. Understand what is most important to product management and use that knowledge when prioritizing. Talk to engineers to understand which fixes are more difficult or complicated than others.

Tackling UX debt will ensure that your product can continue to scale alongside your design system.

Design System Growth

Growing pains can cause daunting challenges, but there are strategies you can use to mitigate risks and take advantage of opportunities. You should think of your system as another team member. It can take on duties and responsibilities, freeing you up to tackle more complicated tasks. The competencies and skills of your design system should grow alongside those of the organization.

Ensure a centralized location for your design system. Make sure that everyone has access. It should pull its weight for the team, answering known questions and allowing other teams the autonomy to work independently.

Stay focused on developing your system. Don't allow delivery pressures and tight timelines to distract you from keeping up with your design system. Your system is an organizational priority. Advocate for it when scheduling and prioritizing work. Make the space for your team to add to and improve its contents continually.

Set up processes and a system of checks and balances. This means a self-documenting design system with designated maintainers tasked with checking the work that is added. Have documentation steps for adding to the system as well as reviewing additions.

Stop trying to make it perfect. Iteration will be vital to keeping your system going. Long, drawn-out conversations about every detail in your system will stop progress and exhaust the team. Get something in and continue to improve it over time.

Iterating on Components and Guidelines

As your organization grows or client needs shift, there will be times when you must iterate on the components and guidelines you have already created. A usage guideline may no longer be useful or a component may have to change entirely to match the needs of your changing product. Don't paint yourself into a corner; keep an open mind and allow your design system to evolve to fit the ever-changing needs of your users.

Making Room for Revisions

Learning to iterate can be a challenge. It is likely that you won't be completely happy with the first iteration of your design system. As you continue to iterate, adding more guidelines often means adding more complexity. Be open to allowing your system to shift over time.

As your product grows and user needs change, so might your guidelines. It is okay to throw out components and begin anew. Remember that your design system is supposed to provide guidance for your team. If a certain guideline is not working within your product anymore, it's time to change or remove it.

Utilizing Research

Research is a powerful tool that will help you to build robust components that function well for your users. Whether you have a team of UX researchers or you're working on your own, you can create small studies that help you test different variations of the same component. Below are a few research techniques that can help you iterate and revise your components to best match your users' needs:

A/B Testing

Performing A/B tests allows you to compare two versions of a component and measure how effective each one is. There are many tools out there to help you easily perform A/B tests, but you can also keep it simple by creating your own prototypes and testing with users one-on-one. This is a powerful tool that helps you determine the most effective iteration of a component.

Usability Testing

If you are unsure whether a certain component will solve a user need, utilize usability testing to get the answers. Start by creating a hypothesis and a list of assumptions. Be clear about what you are hoping to accomplish with your study. Then create a script that you can use when talking with users that addresses your hypothesis and helps answer your assumptions. Be willing to make changes based on the findings within your study.

Beta Groups

When creating a new feature or feature set, you are likely to introduce components into a new flow. Create a beta group to test the new flow before introducing it to the majority of your users. This will also give you useful information regarding whether you need to make any adjustments to your guidelines.

Communicating Changes

A key aspect of revising your design system is ensuring you have a process in place for communicating changes. UX designers should be up to date with the state of your system, as should your engineering team. Keeping your organization in the dark about the changes you make will only lead to inconsistencies and incorrectly implemented components.

When you make a change to a usage guideline, announce the change in your next upcoming team meeting. Remember that when a usage guideline is changed, it may mean updating the implementation of that component. Check in with your engineering team to ensure that the change can be implemented in a timely manner. If there is no capacity to make the change, be sure to document the issue in your issue tracker. This will ensure that the change will be made when scheduling allows. For larger changes that may affect the whole of the organization, be sure to have a channel in place that allows you to communicate the changes to all parties. This will vary between organizations but could be a chat channel, a company call, or a team bulletin.

Tying It All Together

Your design system cannot be completed and then simply set aside. It will require continuous effort and constant attention to thrive. Treat your design system as you would a product. Set goals for what you would like your system to achieve within a specific time frame and track the results. Doing so will allow you to make corrections when necessary and bolster morale for the team as the benefits become clear.

Measuring and tracking results is vital for your stakeholders as well. Provide data that shows the effectiveness of your system and how it is benefiting customer growth and retention. Make clear the value your system has for the organization, and you are more likely to continue receiving support in the form of time and resources.

Maintaining your system as your organization and product grow can be daunting. Create processes to address the addition of team members across the organization and have a plan to tackle UX debt that accumulates.

Account for the need to scale your system in parallel with your product and organization. Start by placing your system in a centralized location and make it available to everyone. Encourage all teams to contribute but reinforce checks and balances. Be open to iteration and create a process for communicating changes over time. Socialize and evangelize your system within the organization to maintain excitement and keep the momentum going.

CHAPTER 7

A GitLab Case Study

Throughout this book, we have combined our collective experiences to share what we've learned while working on design systems throughout our careers. The following case study is a look into our roles, challenges, and successes while working together on the GitLab Design System. Our goal with this chapter is to provide you with concrete experiences from which you can draw parallels while working on your system.

Background

GitLab began as an open source, web-based Git repository manager and quickly grew into a single application for the entire DevOps life cycle. GitLab provides organizations with code, project, and operations management, alongside security and monitoring tooling.

By 2017, GitLab, as an organization and product, was growing fast. We were working on introducing new features while bringing additional designers, engineers, and product managers on board to handle the increase in scope and volume of work. While there was existing markdown documentation in our UX guide, upkeep was manual and time-consuming. The use of static images meant it was prone to being out of date. In addition to a lack of current usage guidelines, our CSS was growing without clear technical guidelines. We had page-specific styles that would cascade down, affecting other areas and producing more interface bugs.

© Sarrah Vesselov and Taurie Davis 2019
S. Vesselov and T. Davis, *Building Design Systems*,
https://doi.org/10.1007/978-1-4842-4514-9_7

Overall, we were lacking two crucial things: reusable components and clear guidelines for their use.

Problem

GitLab was experiencing a growing number of stylistic issues as the product continued to increase in scope. This highlighted consistency concerns. Colors and fonts were not well-defined, and the way we handled components differed from page to page. We found ourselves addressing the same usability problems over and over. The pace of design was slowing, leaving us unable to focus on much beyond the current milestone. Rather than working closely with product managers to generate future features and strategic roadmaps, we found ourselves in a purely transactional role.

With these problems in mind, we needed a way to do the following:

- Increase speed of design and design handoff.

- Improve consistency across GitLab.

- Make time for exploratory UX work and discovery.

- Empower the entire company to make design decisions.

- Speed up and improve the quality of onboarding.

Our Roles

To understand how we worked together to create GitLab's design system, we thought it would be helpful to begin by giving an overview of our roles. While we both contributed to all aspects of planning, building, and evangelizing our system, it was necessary for each of us to own a specific part of the effort. Doing so allowed each of us to concentrate our efforts and avoid getting pulled in too many directions.

Sarrah

Sarrah's primary role was to gain support and buy-in from stakeholders, as well as remove any obstacles that stood in the department's way. The first and most crucial stakeholder was the design department itself. While we all knew there was a need for a dedicated design system, there were many obstacles for the design department to consider before we could begin.

Our department was doing all it could to stay on top of monthly deliverables, and our capacity was maxed. Hiring dedicated designers to work on our system was not an option, meaning we had to make time by taking on fewer deliverables each month. For this to happen effectively, we needed to socialize with each product manager the reasons why. Their understanding and support were vital.

Sarrah also ensured that the design system effort was supported by the design department's Object and Key Results (OKRs). This meant gaining support from the CEO and VP of Engineering while making sure the department prioritized the efforts that supported each key result. These OKRs proved to be vital in ensuring that the department was focused on and committed to the design system.

Choosing which technology to use was also a challenge. There were varying opinions on which tools and technology were best-suited to the department. We spent a lot of time talking about what we should use. Sarrah pushed for a decision and made sure that one person was driving the effort. There was no way she could get buy-in from the designers, product managers, engineers, and executives while also navigating the many choices that needed to be made about tooling. Taurie stepped up to own this responsibility, acting as a guide and point of pressure on the department.

We had an existing UX guide in the company-wide GitLab handbook, the central location for all of our documentation. However, this was not the best location for our design system. We knew that we needed the ability to house documentation alongside working components and CSS styles.

113

The decision was easy to make on the department level, but we needed to present a strong argument for why it had to be a standalone resource.

Much of Sarrah's time was spent socializing the system with the CEO, head of product, VP of Engineering, and other engineering managers. It was imperative that these stakeholders understood the benefits the system would bring to GitLab. Having their support from the start would make it easier to gain buy-in from the rest of the organization. Sarrah also spent time evangelizing the design system, sharing it with GitLab as well as the larger community.

Taurie

While Sarrah worked to gain support and remove obstacles, Taurie drove the implementation of the design system. At the start, the design department had no formal component library to utilize, and we wanted to begin thinking about design as a scalable system. As the department and product continued to grow, it was apparent that we needed clear guidelines that would help direct us toward making consistent design decisions.

Taurie began by determining the best way to build a component library that the design department could contribute to easily. A key aspect for her was to find something that was reliable and easy to understand—a tool that would allow any new designer to come in and familiarize themselves with our design language on day one.

Taurie set up the foundation for the department to build upon, aiding designers in developing a component library that contained styles and components used on a regular basis. With the component library in place, she was able to shift her focus to building the design system. Taurie recruited members of the front-end department who showed an interest in the system and were able to assist along the way. The goal at this time was the same as when we began the component library: create a foundation from which the entire department could build.

The design system began as a series of components and guidelines grouped into specific categories, many of which we have covered in this book. While the pages of our system began as placeholder to-dos, the critical thing for us was to create a vision that the department could run with themselves. With a defined structure and information hierarchy, we were able to start writing UX documentation together. The entire design department contributed to filling in to-dos every month.

Taurie began to work closely with Sarrah to communicate the benefits of a design system and how it would help improve productivity. It was imperative to get the support of the front-end engineering department in order to include working components within our system. Over time, we shaped a shared vision of our design system that enabled both departments to work together. At this point, we were able to begin building a series of repositories that integrate, with the goal of feeding both our design system and the product as a single source of truth.

Challenges

As with many companies setting out to build a design system, there were challenges and constraints that cropped up along the way. While some were within our direct control, many were not. As each new obstacle came up, we were challenged to evaluate the situation and set a course for resolution. The following outlines the struggles we encountered, our approach to solving them, and the resulting outcome.

Misconceptions and Buy-In

Design systems were a new concept to a lot of team members at GitLab when we first began. We knew that we would have to educate our peers on what a design system was, as well as what it wasn't. A common misconception we encountered often was that the design system would simply house usability guidelines. We had to be diligent, communicating the full scope of a design system to ensure we had proper support throughout the process. Gaining stakeholder buy-in would enable us to make further headway and align teams along a common goal.

Our Approach

We began with our direct supervisor, discussing the advantages a design system would bring to the organization. We detailed the speed and consistency benefits it would afford the design department, as well as engineering. Fortunately, it wasn't a tough sell. Design reports directly to the VP of Engineering, and our supervisor understood the value a design system would bring to the organization as a whole.

During this time, we reached out to the engineering managers in the front-end department. Again, we focused on communicating the benefits this would have for both engineering and design.

It took time to communicate the full scope of a design system and get everyone on the same page. We became comfortable addressing misconceptions. We knew that if context was missing, it would lead to misunderstandings about what a design system was meant to accomplish. On a consistent basis, we made an effort to ensure everyone understood and agreed with the primary goals a design system would solve. This also meant revisiting technical implementation strategies as different people were brought into the discussion.

The next step was to gain support from the product department. At GitLab, product managers set the road map and prioritization for each milestone. If we were going to make any headway on our system, we would have to take on fewer deliverables each month. While speed and consistency are indeed concerns for product managers, it was difficult to make this case while intentionally slowing down the work they wanted to accomplish. Here, we needed to do our best to align our design system efforts with the product roadmap. We prioritized components that tied directly into the issues that mapped to the product department's vision and strategy. In this way, the problems we were already working on could be used to drive what we were adding to the system.

Outcome

As a shared vision developed over time, we were able to gain more buy-in. With the front-end engineering department on board, we were able to dovetail our design system efforts nicely into engineering efforts to introduce Vue components and refactor CSS. Rather than go it alone, we were able to work together, pushing for a single source of truth for the entire organization. In addition to working closely with engineering, we worked in parallel with product. This ensured that we were able to execute on our monthly deliverables while also writing guidelines for our newly defined components.

Resourcing

Finding the people and time to start our design system was a significant challenge. As a department, we were already ruthlessly prioritizing the work we needed to accomplish each month. We had been working with the rest of the department to allocate time toward documenting our existing components but there wasn't the necessary time or people to devote to the system. Additionally, we faced challenges in getting working code components embedded into our system as we could not control, or even influence, the front-end resources available to assist us.

Our Approach

As with everything at GitLab, we started with an issue. Issues allow you to share and discuss proposals before and during implementation. This was the first step toward rallying resources within the design department.

The issue description[1] contained the following excerpt:

Let's focus on the Big picture for GitLab's UX. It is important that we keep our day to day work focused on contributing to larger goals. It is easy to get so heads down in our work that we lose sight of bigger things we are trying to accomplish as a team and company.

This issue intends to set UX goals that will continue to establish and evolve GitLab's UX. We already have OKRs for this quarter, and those will need to be considered in determining which issues to take up and move forward with. However, I think there is plenty of room for us to focus on UX centric goals. Specifically, cleaning up and establishing GitLab's unique personality and voice.

The basic ground rules are:

- *Each team member should think about an area they would want to focus on and contribute to*

- *We must be sure to support our OKRs fully*

- *We should write a blog post (or series of) stating our plan—declare our intentions to the community and company*

- *All issues we take on and create should support our plan*

- *We should establish a GitLab Pages[2] for UX (`design.gitlab.com`)—Be visibly committed*

The end goal is to have an established UX Foundation Guide.

---

[1]Sarrah Vesselov, "[META] UX Big Plan," `https://gitlab.com/gitlab-org/gitlab-design/issues/30`.

[2]Pages is a feature that allows you to publish websites for your repositories within GitLab.

This issue description was the starting point for our design system. It committed us to dedicating time to work on the system at the department level. Making time for the necessary work we needed to do highlighted our lack of resources overall. With no dedicated team, we were delivering less toward the product road map and struggling to make significant progress on our system. We highlighted this as a case for hiring additional UX designers.

We used OKRs as another strategy to assemble resources. GitLab uses OKRs as a way to inspire and drive teams to push forward essential initiatives. We sought to guarantee time dedicated to our system by driving key results related to these efforts. This required support from the CEO himself, but we were met with some resistance. The perception was that an OKR should be focused on initiatives outside of an individual's job responsibilities, and the design system did not meet this requirement. We explained that the value of a design system went beyond individual job responsibilities. By leveraging key results, we could ensure the system was included and prioritized with other initiatives. We needed a forcing function if we were going to make progress. In the end, we were able to dedicate the design system as part of our OKRs for two quarters.

Outcome

We unified the design department through a shared vision using a familiar way of working. Opening an issue allowed us to branch off, creating more issues and dividing up work. It encouraged the department to have more discussions and come together around solidified goals. In supporting our design system through the use of OKRs, we were able to ensure that designers could devote time toward building the component library and documenting usage guidelines. Doing so set the stage for designers to get in the habit of carving out space for the design system. Even after the system was no longer an OKR, designers continued to include at least one design system issue as a deliverable during each release cycle.

Tooling

When we set out to build our component library, we were already using Sketch[3] as our primary design tool at GitLab. Although we evaluated other software, it was natural for us to continue using a familiar tool. However, Sketch team libraries had not yet been released, and the process of selecting a tool to facilitate the creation and use of a synced team library proved more difficult than initially anticipated. We evaluated several tools available and encountered various problems, such as:

- Slow performance, as well as bugs, when adding, changing, and renaming components.

- Limited Sketch capabilities, such as not including override options when adding symbols[4] to a new document.

- Frustrating bugs, such as text styles that weren't saved or included within symbols.

Our Approach

We knew that if we continued to evaluate every tool available, we would never make progress on our component library. To solve the issue of managing shared assets, we assessed the top tools that were available at the time and decided to move forward with Brand.ai. This Sketch plugin solved many of the technical issues we were running into with other tools, but no tool is perfect:

---

[3]Sketch is a vector-based design tool that allows you to create mockups and prototypes for user interfaces.

[4]Symbols are a feature within Sketch that allow you to reuse the same component across different files. Updating the master symbol will apply the changes to every instance of that symbol. You can also use overrides to make changes to the symbol used in a specific instance.

- Our complex product benefited from various levels of nesting, and Brand.ai limited the organization of components to only one level deep.

- While faster and less buggy than other plugins, Brand.ai was slow and becoming slower as more components were added.

The department has since moved away from using Brand.ai and switched to native Sketch libraries. We made this change only after making sure it would improve our workflow and not set us back in terms of build out. Ultimately, it was clear to the department that the new Sketch feature would improve our overall workflow and ensure that we could iterate faster toward a more complete component library.

Outcome

By being flexible with tooling, the department was able to focus on building robust and reusable components. We only switched tools when it made sense for the team and would not hinder our progress. This meant that we could define guidelines for our components and build them out with more speed, ensuring that we met our OKRs and maintained our stakeholders' buy-in.

Structure and Setup

When we first began work on the design system, we struggled with how it would be structured from a technical perspective. We knew that everything would have to be integrated, but we had to work within the various resourcing constraints to make that happen. With limited front-end resources, this meant getting started with whatever project setup we could. We knew we would have to figure out how our working components would be integrated into the system, as well as the actual product, at a later date.

Our Approach

In the early stages, we sought out members of the front-end department to help us determine how to structure the system from a technical perspective. As a fully remote company, GitLab is distributed globally across more than 40 countries. We took advantage of one of our annual work summits, where we gathered in person for a week, to meet with two front-end engineers who showed interest in helping start the design system. Getting their input and assistance at this very early stage enabled us to make headway on building an outward-facing design system. They proved to be valuable allies after we returned home by answering questions and assisting with technical implementation going forward.

One of our strengths throughout this project was the ability to iterate toward a robust design system. Iteration encouraged members of various departments to get involved throughout the process. We didn't keep the design system locked away until it was ready for a successful launch. Instead, we shipped a blank canvas with an extensive list of placeholder to-dos, shown in Figure 7-1, that could be filled in over time by various team members. The addition of a component status page informed users, at a glance, which components were ready and which still needed documentation.

Tables

Design   Vue Component

This component's documentation has not yet been added.

Related patterns

No related patterns known.

Figure 7-1. *By creating blank pages with to-dos, team members could quickly see which areas still required documentation*

Outcome

Recognizing peers who are interested in helping you build your system is invaluable. Dedicating time to talk with members of the front-end team allowed us to propel our design system forward. Even though we didn't have the ability to add engineering resources, we had formed allies whom we could ask for help along the way.

With a shared vision of the design system among departments, we filled in the blank slate we'd created with the help of our front-end allies. We made steady progress each month, by scheduling components at three distinct levels:

- Documenting usage guidelines.

- Wrapping existing components and writing styles.

- Implementing new components within the product.

Having these three levels in place allowed designers and engineers to work on the design system in tandem.

Component Redundancy: Buttons, Badges, Labels, Tags, Oh My!

GitLab is a complex product with many features that span the entire DevOps life cycle. There is an abundance of components to organize, document, and implement within a product so involved. Working on the design system forced the department to sit down and define specifics for each component. We realized we had many visually similar interface elements being used in varying contexts.

An excellent example of this was our use of buttons, badges, labels, and tags, as shown in Figure 7-2. Although some were informational, interactive, or both, they were using virtually the same styling without clearly defined usage guidelines. It wasn't clear when to use one vs. another.

Figure 7-2. *Visually similar components that lacked clear usage guidelines*

Our Approach

Sitting down to define each component meant that we had to recognize the similarities, identify the differences, combine duplicates, and establish usage guidelines. As illustrated in Figure 7-3, we ultimately were able to reduce the number of components, simplifying when and where to use each one.

Figure 7-3. *After determining clear usage guidelines, we were able to reduce the number of total components while also giving each one a visually unique style*

To arrive at this outcome, one designer took ownership of determining a solution to the problem we had identified. We then followed a standard code review process.[5] This review process ensures that any changes made

---

[5]GitLab, "Code Review," `https://about.gitlab.com/handbook/engineering/` `workflow/code-review/`.

are reviewed before they are introduced into the product. We adopted this process of checks and balances, tasking designers with reviewing all changes that were made to both the component library and the design system.

In addition to having reviewers, we also had a set of maintainers. While everyone is encouraged to help review changes, only maintainers are able to accept changes to the design system. Maintainers are subject matter experts and know the codebase extremely well, enabling them to spot inconsistencies or problems that could be easily missed by others.

Outcome

With reviewers and maintainers in place, we created a robust process that is less likely to introduce bugs or inconsistencies to our design system. This minimized mistakes and broadened the scope of knowledge across the organization by getting more eyes on changes early. It allowed us to work collaboratively toward the best solution, providing feedback along the way.

Communicating Value

For a long time, the work of the design department at GitLab went largely under the radar, both internally and externally. That isn't to say that our peers at GitLab did not value and appreciate our work. They did, and do. However, the bulk of our work and accomplishments were a part of the whole, in which product managers presented designs and solutions in the monthly kickoff call. We often faced criticism, largely for being transactional in our work rather than focusing on thinking strategically and generating ideas for the product. All of this took a toll on the morale of the team, and it was something we needed to change.

After working on the design system for nearly a year, the design department felt good about the progress we had made. Everything in the original UX guide was moved from the handbook over to our dedicated site, `design.gitlab.com`. We documented many new components while old components were being revisited and updated. As a department, the design system was our single source of truth for information on components and how to use them. We had written blog posts about the design system that garnered attention from the broader UX community, and we were seeing applicants citing it as a reason for applying. Designers had more time to dedicate to generating ideas and working toward the product road map. While we were still waiting for the capacity required to implement working code components, we felt that our efforts had paid off.

However, in a conversation with one executive, we received feedback that the system was a failure. This opinion was formed because, from their perspective, nobody was using it. You can imagine our surprise and disappointment when we heard this. The design department was using the system on a daily basis as part of our work, and the front-end department was just beginning to add the corresponding code components. How could this perception be so different from ours?

Our Approach

We quickly realized that, while the system was a daily part of our lives, we had not yet made it part of the daily lives of the organization as a whole. In this regard, we had failed. We immediately set about correcting this. First, we added announcements about the design system in the company call, weekly engineering newsletter, and product management meetings. Next, we ensured that reviewing the design system was part of onboarding for all front-end engineers and product managers. We added a dedicated company chat channel for our design system and shared it with the entire organization. Finally, we created buzz and excitement by branding the system with its own name and styling. All of these efforts helped us to communicate the worth of the system to the entire company, ultimately broadening its audience.

Outcome

The design system needed championing to be successful. We needed to engage in activities that highlighted our work, our struggles, and our successes. We talked about it in company calls, slack channels, in blog posts, and in a webinar dedicated to showcasing how we work together remotely. We added our design system additions to our kickoff call, highlighting our efforts and contributions.

These efforts paid off. We saw an increase in overall engagement from other departments within GitLab. We also saw an increase in engagement with the broader UX community. Designers around the world were sharing our posts, providing feedback, and applying to our open remote positions.

Lessons Learned

Throughout the process of implementing a design system at GitLab, we learned many valuable lessons. For example, remember that reiterating goals often ensures that teams are working toward a shared vision. Align your efforts with the goals that other teams have set out to accomplish. This allows both of you to make progress, guaranteeing your efforts won't be sidelined. We also learned that utilizing your company's way of measuring initiatives can be extremely effective in ensuring that your department has the necessary time to devote to your objective.

We learned that gathering allies is very beneficial, especially when resources are tight or nonexistent. Working iteratively will ensure that you can set a foundation from which to build over time, getting help along the way when needed.

Throughout this process, we came to understand that tools are continually transforming and that frequently changing them will slow progress. We learned to evaluate tools carefully and decide what is best for the team at the current moment. Remember that component libraries and design tools are only one aspect that helps you arrive at a design system.

Creating a series of checks and balances ensures your work is being reviewed by colleagues. This strengthens the overall output and ensures that you are considering all use cases when documenting new guidelines or creating new components.

Last, we learned that celebrating the successes, no matter how small they may seem, is vital to keeping the momentum going. Even as we faced a variety of challenges, we were able to make progress in critical areas. Recognize and share the successes throughout your organization and you'll be prepared to overcome the next obstacle that comes your way.

Next Steps

We can't say it enough: building your design system is a continual process. While many of our original goals and objectives have been met, the effort to scale and adapt the system to meet the changing needs of GitLab continues. After the progress made over the first year and a half of building GitLab's system, we were left with some additional initiatives. This included ensuring that the system was the primary location for not only product guidelines but all things related to marketing as well. We also wanted to move designers away from their reliance on design software by utilizing the design system as a means of working more closely with production code.

Marketing

Marketing guidelines were not an original aspect of our design system. At GitLab, the design department is separate from the designers working on the informational website and marketing materials. While we remain in close proximity, our day-to-day work is very different. As GitLab grows and expands, it is critical to maintain a consistent brand experience across the product and marketing material. We established the information architecture to support branding and product guidelines, as seen in Figure 7-4. Our end goal is to work with the marketing design team to move all of the marketing documentation over to the design system in an effort to create one cohesive experience.

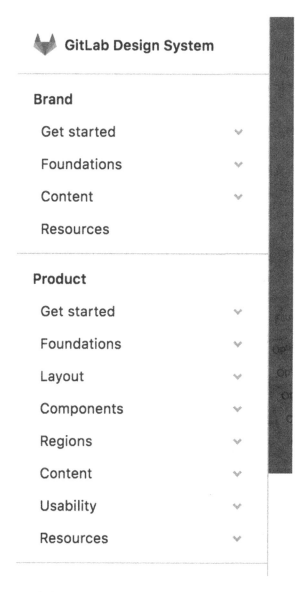

Figure 7-4. *Guidelines are broken down into brand and product sections*

Less Reliance on Design Tools

One of our original goals was to enable our design department to think in terms of systems. What we ship to production is what our users will see, not the mocks and prototypes we create in various design tools. Relying on these programs to translate user flows separates designers from the actual user experience. Design systems empower members of various departments to work more closely to the shipped product and, in turn, the users of that product.

We began this journey by creating a component library within Sketch. However, that was just one step in a series of steps that led us to the design system we have today. As we continue to build our design system, the ultimate goal is to iterate away from relying on design tools and empower designers to work more closely with the production code. Iterating toward this workflow will enable designers to easily prototype in the browser, using cleanly documented, reusable components that will be directly used within the end-user environment.

Tying It All Together

Significant progress was made on GitLab's design system over the span of a year and a half. There was still work to be done, but the benefits of our system were felt across the organization, even in the early stages. We saw the design system begin to accomplish the goals we were aiming to achieve at the very beginning of this process.

Increased speed of design and design handoff. Although the effort is ongoing, we saw an increase in efficiency related to delivering designs to the engineering department. Designers are able to consult guidelines in the design phase and link to them when handing them off to an engineer.

Improved consistency across GitLab. We documented style and usage guidelines in order to improve consistency throughout the product. This allowed us to align elements and components, such as colors, fonts, dropdowns, and forms. Problem areas that still existed were identified and placed on the road map for future improvements.

More time for exploratory UX work and discovery. While this was a challenging goal to accomplish, we saw improvements. Having standardized guidelines gave the department breathing room to think less about designing UI elements and focus more time on strategic thinking and problem solving.

Empowers the entire company to make design decisions. The design system has been shared and promoted to the whole organization. Product managers and engineers use it to guide them in making suggestions for user experience improvements. They don't have to wait for a designer to become available, they can propose a solution themselves, using the system as a guide.

Increased speed and quality of onboarding. The design system has been added to the list of onboarding resources for product managers, designers, and front-end engineers. It has aided new team members in familiarizing themselves with the product and our vision for building it.

Iterating toward a robust design system allowed us to make headway on the goals we set out to achieve. As in any company, we faced a series of challenges that we had to overcome along the way. While these can be frustrating at times, it is important to not give up. Keep sight of your goals, and your efforts will pay off.

CHAPTER 8

Design Systems As a Resource

Starting your own design system can be overwhelming. While we've provided you with everything you need to start working, it can be helpful to look at existing systems for inspiration. Public-facing and open source design systems provide a window into how different organizations categorize and structure their systems. In this chapter, we will cover the common similarities and differences you can expect to encounter among popular design systems when researching for your own.

The Role of Open Source

The term *open source* refers to publicly available technology that is often free to use and modify. The goal of open source software is to encourage and maintain free-flowing ideas, unhindered by proprietary business interests. Open source projects are developed and curated by those with a deep interest in the software, as well as the problem that software seeks to solve. This interest helps contribute to higher quality, as the goals revolve around the software itself, rather than potential monetary gain.

Open source software (OSS) also helped contribute to the open design movement. While open design often refers to physical products, the principles remain the same as OSS. Primarily, this involves publicly

© Sarrah Vesselov and Taurie Davis 2019
S. Vesselov and T. Davis, *Building Design Systems*,
https://doi.org/10.1007/978-1-4842-4514-9_8

sharing design information related to the development of your product and allowing anyone to use and alter it freely.[1]

These trends have encouraged companies to be more open with their design language. Many organizations have even created and open-sourced their design systems as a way of disseminating information more efficiently. It has allowed organizations to get direct feedback and contributions from users, as well as designers and engineers working with their system. Access to these systems has provided an easy way to learn the reasoning behind decisions made, enabling designers to improve the user experience while collaborating more effectively with engineers.

Google's Material Design debuted in 2014 and was backed by open source code. It provided stronger dialogue and improved collaboration among designers and developers, as each group had insight into the function as well as the form of the product.

Throughout this chapter, we will use publicly available design systems as a way of researching common similarities and differences. Use these as an additional way to understand what is essential to include in your system, but remember that every organization is unique and will have different needs and goals.

Researching Other Systems

Looking at how other organizations tackle their design systems is helpful when starting your own. It is also often overwhelming. We found that there are many design systems out there, all with their own way of categorizing, organizing, and conveying their design language. It is challenging to know which method makes the most sense for your system.

---

[1]AdCiv.org, "Open collaborative design," http://www.adciv.org/Open_collaborative_design, last updated July 29, 2010.

Rather than look at other systems as a prescription for how a design system should be, look to them for insight and inspiration. You will notice many similarities and just as many differences. At first, it can be difficult to grasp the reasons behind why they differ. Why does one system use *voice and tone* while others use *writing style*? Why do some systems break things down into elements and components while others don't? Much of the differences come down to what we have focused on throughout this book: the size of the organization, the type of product it builds, organizational needs, and user goals. Study these systems as an additional way of understanding what makes the most sense for your organization.

It is important to remember that these systems, like all, are in constant evolution. By the time you are reading this, they have likely undergone additional tweaks and changes.

Commonalities

Nearly every system contains the essentials: typography, grid, color, components, etc. Some include general guidelines for components with more specific usage guidelines for each component group. This is necessary because specific rules come out of combined groups that do not exist for the individual components. Many also include working code examples, along with technical guidelines.

It is common for design systems to include particular guidelines to describe and prescribe personality, voice, and tone. These typically consist of a word or short phrase, such as "Playful" or "Optimistic," followed by a few guiding sentences that set the tone for the brand.

Most systems do not include a section specific to marketing. Atlassian and GitLab are the only organizations that have a separate section dedicated to marketing guidelines within their systems. Including marketing in your design system can strengthen the alignment between the user experience of the product and how that product is branded and marketed to users.

Some systems supply users and possible contributors with access to resources such as code repositories, design files, and icon sets. They often include user-friendly public-facing sites focused on both design and development. These sites help foster design thinking within your organization.

Differences

We saw a distinct difference between design systems in how they choose to build and mix elements. Some systems, such as Google's Material Design, use design standards similar to those of Atomic design.[2] Atomic design is defined by breaking interfaces down into basic building blocks and working up from there. Every piece of the interface must be defined.

Other systems, such as Airbnb's Design Language System (DLS) and IBM take a different approach. They don't break components down into atoms, because they believe this allows too many permutations. Instead, they define individual components that work together within an ecosystem.[3] For Airbnb, this maintains their brand, even as they make adjustments for the many different cultures and languages they support. At IBM, this approach helps them remain consistent across their platforms. The differences can be subtle. This is how Airbnb's design team describes the differences:

> *Instead of relying on individual atoms (or atomic design), we started considering our components as elements of a living organism. They have a function and personality, are defined by a set of properties, can co-exist with others and can evolve (or*

---

[2]Brad Frost, "Atomic Design," http://atomicdesign.bradfrost.com/.

[3]Karri Saarinen, "Building a Visual Language," https://airbnb.design/building-a-visual-language/.

die) independently. This is one of the key points about the system compared to more atomic ones—we don't have complicated networks of interconnected parts and components.

—Karri Saarinen[4]

Further differences arise in how organizations choose to categorize and structure their systems. A few begin with guiding principles, working progressively toward elements and components.

Atlassian and GitLab split their systems into marketing and product sections before listing guiding principles, elements, and components. Mailchimp does not include any guiding principles.

There is a variety of terminology used by different systems. Some use the terms *patterns* and *components*. However, in Shopify's system, the pattern section includes guidelines for layout, error messages, and mobile patterns, while their components section is dedicated to reusable interface elements. Mailchimp's system combines patterns and components under the general term *patterns*, providing guidelines and code snippets together. GitLab makes a distinction between components and regions, with regions representing overarching design paradigms such as the navigation. Other organizations refer to these paradigms as patterns. Most systems include guidelines for overarching paradigms, but the naming often varies. While the terminology differs, the contents remain similar and often overlap.

Table 8-1 provides an overview of some of the more well-known design systems. It illustrates, at a high level, the commonalities and differences you will encounter. The structure and terminology can differ wildly from system to system. We suggest that when researching other systems, don't become overwhelmed by nomenclature. When you feel lost, review this book as a guide. Remember to remain focused on the needs of your organization and be consistent in how you apply terminology within your system.

---

[4]Karri Saarinen, "Airbnb—Design Language System," https://karrisaarinen. com/dls/.

Table 8-1. *Overview of the Contents Within Some of the More Popular Design Systems*

	Atlassian	Firefox (Photon)	Mailchimp	Shopify (Polaris)	IBM (Carbon)	Google (Material)	GitLab (Pajamas)
Open source							
Public-facing	✓	✓	✓	✓	✓	✓	✓
Repository	✓	✓		✓		✓	✓
Layout							
Grid/Spacing	✓	✓	✓	✓	✓	✓	✓
Styles							
Typography	✓	✓	✓	✓	✓	✓	✓
Color	✓	✓	✓	✓	✓	✓	✓
Iconography	✓	✓	✓	✓	✓	✓	✓
Sound				✓			
Motion		✓			✓	✓	✓
Interaction				✓	✓	✓	✓
Illustration	✓	✓		✓			✓
Components							
with code	✓		✓	✓	✓	✓	✓
without code		✓					
Patterns/Regions							
...	✓	✓		✓	✓		✓
Content							
Voice & Tone	✓	✓		✓		✓	✓
Writing Style/Copy	✓	✓		✓		✓	✓
Usability							
Internationalization				✓			
Accessibility	✓	✓		✓		✓	✓
Resources							
Design Files	✓			✓	✓	✓	✓
Design Blog		✓			✓	✓	
Development Blog	✓	✓			✓	✓	
Fonts		✓		✓		✓	
Icons (SVG)	✓	✓	✓	✓	✓	✓	✓
Logos	✓	✓	✓				✓
Miscellaneous							
Marketing	✓						✓
Design principles		✓		✓	✓	✓	✓
Design tokens		✓					
Theming				✓	✓	✓	

138

Tying It All Together

The systems we've outlined all contain key aspects that help drive their individual design languages. What works for them won't necessarily be a good fit for your organization. Use these design systems, along with this book, as a reference and inspiration for when you feel lost or unsure of which direction to go in.

Index

A

A/B testing, 107
Accessibility, 77, 82, 83, 88, 95
    Voluntary Product Accessibility
        Template (VPAT), 83
Agile methodology, 10
Assessing organization, 47, 63
    organization age, 17
    stakeholder buy-in, 65
    team size, 18, 65
    volume and work type, 18

B

Bauhaus design
    movement, 2
Beta group, 107

C

Card-sorting, 70–71
Code review, 94, 124
Communication strategies, 44
    diplomacy, 44–45
    education, 45
    good PR, 47
    salesmanship, 46–47
Component, 14, 52
    building, 53, 80
    groups, 14
    library, 15–16, 19, 79, 130
Content, 82
CSS, 5, 7, 85, 117

D

Data gathering
    goal setting, 94–95
    survey, 96
    survey template, 96–102
    UX team survey, 99
Designer Persona, *see* Personas
Design language
    attributes, 51–52
    design principles, 59
Design Language System (DLS), 136
Design principles, 16
    definition, 59
    practical guide, 60–62
Design system
    communication strategies, 44
    value, dimension, 26 (*see also*
        Value, dimension of)
    worksheet, 47–49
Design system failures, 20–22
Design tools, 79–80, 120–121

Printed in the United States
By Bookmasters